giggle guide to
baby gear

giggle guide to
baby gear

ali wing | text by **mariella krause**

illustrations by **arthur mount**

CHRONICLE BOOKS
SAN FRANCISCO

Library of Congress Cataloging-in-Publication Data: wing, ali.
   giggle guide to baby gear: the smart shopping companion for new
   parents / ali wing; text by mariella krause; illustrations by arthur mount.
   p. cm. includes index. isbn 978-0-8118-6197-7 (alk. paper)

   1. infants--care. 2. infants' supplies--purchasing. 3. consumer education. i. krause, mariella. ii. title. rj61.w66 2008 • 649'.1220284--dc22 •
   2007044189

ISBN: 978-0-8118-6197-7

10 9 8 7 6 5 4 3 2 1

Design by: **www.rise-and-shinestudio.com**
Manufactured in China.

Chronicle Books LLC
680 Second Street
San Francisco, California 94107
www.chroniclebooks.com

CONTENTS

CHECKLISTS

1 expecting parents

- learning: building your parenting library
- pampering: taking care of the mom-to-be
- nesting: setting up the nursery
- the big day: coming home from the hospital

2 the first six months

- basics: tools for everyday living
- clothing: your baby basics
- nursing: the original liquid diet
- diapering: time for a change
- bathing: get ready for tub-time
- teething: soothing secrets

3 toddlerhood

- growing: bigger baby, different stuff
- eating: introducing real food
- potty training: graduating diapers
- safety-proofing: getting the house ready

4 getting out and about

- traveling: arriving with your sanity intact
- outdoors: fun in the sun
- weather: getting out in the snow and rain

PRODUCTS

5 baby on the go

- car seats
- strollers
- baby carriers
- diaper bags

6 the nursery

- cribs and beds
- nursery linens
- changing tables
- rockers and gliders
- baby monitors

7 feeding

- bottles and nipples
- breast pumps
- feeding support pillows
- high chairs
- dishes
- bibs

8 bath time

- bathtubs
- skin- and hair-care

introduction:
we're here to help!

Welcome to parenthood! It's an exciting time (as anyone will tell you), but it's also easy to feel overwhelmed (which not everyone will tell you).

There's so much to think about. What will we name the baby? Will I be a good parent? How will it change my life?

And then there's all that stuff you've got to buy. What do you need? Where do you start? And where are you going to put it all?

Yes, shopping for a new baby can be a tremendous task. Anyone who's ever walked into a baby superstore can relate to the feeling of staring at a wall of 50 different car seats, each one indistinguishable from the next. With the explosion of baby products on the market, the choices are endless, and it's hard to make an informed decision about every single item you need to purchase.

Once you've gone through it, it all seems perfectly easy. But when you're making those decisions for the first time, you might find yourself wondering what you'll really need, when you'll need it, and where you need to go to have the secret microchip implanted that will equip you to make the right choices.

Unfortunately, a lot of parents get their education the hard way: through trial and error. Many new parents end up buying things they don't need, only finding out after it's too late what they should have bought instead. Thus, garages all across our country are piled high with purchasing experiments that didn't quite stick: furniture the kids outgrew too quickly, the stroller that didn't hold up to urban living, the sling that was quickly replaced by a traditional baby carrier. . . . The list goes on.

Luckily, there are plenty of parents who have come before you, and there's no shortage of advice. We talk to parents every single day in our stores, and we know what things they can't live without and what items they bought and never used. And that's why it's going to be different for you. With the help of this book, you can make a clear plan and lots of smart decisions.

In the first section, you'll find a series of checklists that will tell you everything you'll need. We've broken these checklists down by stage so you can take it one step at a time, at your own speed. Then, in the second section, we'll help you understand what types of products to look for to match your needs and lifestyle, so you can find the right fit the first time out.

There are plenty of advice books on the market for new parents that aim to help them understand parenting and development. There are also gear guides that explain the specific features of different makes and models of everything from cribs to car seats. This book lives somewhere in between: it's an advice book focused on gear. Before you can choose a model based on a random list of features, you have to understand how to approach the decision and understand what features will actually be important to you—something most people don't find out until they've already made that decision. By giving you a lens through which to filter your decision-making, you can make an informed choice and pick the very best products for your needs.

You've already taken a step in the right direction. You're doing your research and arming yourself with information to make the right decisions. Which means less stress for you—and less money spent on things you'll never use.

the abundance of choices

In the past twenty years, there's been an explosion of baby products. In the "good" old days, a car seat was pretty much optional, and no one gave their stroller much thought as long as it came with four wheels and a handle. Style was pretty much unheard of; baby products came in a strict palette of powdery pastels, and a fashion choice meant, "With teddy bears or without?"

But things have changed. You have choices available to you that your parents never dreamed of. In fact, a lot of grandparents these days are amused by all the things we think we can't live without. After all, you didn't have them when you were a baby, and you turned out just fine, didn't you?

In a way, they have a point. There are tons of options, and a good percentage of them are completely unnecessary. On the other hand, there are a lot of innovations that can make your new job as a parent easier, more fun, and (if you're lucky) less expensive.

Some of the things you can live without will be pretty obvious. You know if you're the kind of person who needs a deluxe potty-training seat with a built-in toilet-paper holder, or if a regular old potty seat will do. You have an instinct for whether you're the heated baby wipe kind. And buying a set of man breasts—well, that's a decision that's purely personal.

But beyond those products that are more novelty than necessity, there are still lots of meaningful decisions to be made. Even though the choices may be overwhelming, we can all agree that this plethora of options has led to a vastly improved quality of life.

For one thing, there have been huge technological improvements that really make a difference, such as high-tech breast pumps that make going back to work a little easier, pacifiers that dispense medicine and take temperatures, and baby monitors that actually work.

Another big improvement is in the area of travel. Parents on the go can now take advantage of travel-friendly items that just weren't available to our parents. And now you don't have to be one of those parents at the airport that everybody feels sorry for, lugging around half a nursery while trying to soothe an anxious child.

Nowadays, if you spend more, you can expect more. In the past, expensive items were luxury items, such as sterling-silver spoons, cashmere blankets, or a really expensive pram that didn't *do* more but did *cost* more. Today, your money gets you innovation, features, and quality. For example, you can get a stroller that evolves from a bassinet to an every-day stroller, monitors that also work as nanny-cams, and a single piece of furniture that goes from a bassinet to a crib to a toddler bed.

You also have a lot more choices when it comes to style. Products are designed with a more contemporary feel and come in a wider range of styles and colors (in case powder pink and baby blue don't happen to be your favorite colors).

Because there are so many choices, actually choosing can be a daunting task—especially since you want everything to be perfect. But if you arm yourself with enough research, you can use the abundance of choices to your advantage, rather than just becoming overwhelmed by them.

the decision-making process

The first half of this book tells you what you need, and the second half tells you how to pick everything out. We'll address each of the different categories of baby gear, such as car seats, cribs, and diaper bags. And in each section, we'll guide you through the process of narrowing down your options one step at a time.

First, we'll give you a category overview. Then, we'll walk you through your basic choices—in other words, the overall types available. Next, we'll offer our general purchasing advice in this category, and then take you through a list of features you might encounter while shopping. This will help you understand what each of the features are and whether or not you'll need them, so that when you're looking at a product description in the store, it will mean something to you.

We'll then narrow the field further by explaining what age of child, or *stage*, the gear is aimed toward. When can I start using it? How long will I use it? Do I use it differently for different ages? Or do I have to buy different styles for different ages? Finally, we'll call out special considerations based on your lifestyle, offer tips for usage, and list the accessories you might want to buy to get the most out of your purchase.

understanding your lifestyle

Here's the thing about recommendations: they're all relative. And that doesn't mean you should only take advice from relatives; it means that what your best friend thinks is the *best thing ever invented* could end up sitting unused in your garage. Why the discrepancy? Is it because some parents are smarter than others? Not at all. It's because everyone is different.

Take strollers. Say your best friend drives a great big SUV and mostly takes her stroller to the mall, while you live up two flights of stairs and barely have room for the baby, let alone bulky equipment. Chances are, you'll look for very different features. The best products for you are those that fit the way you live; the key to knowing what will work for you is finding out what worked for people *like* you.

There are six lifestyle categories that should be taken into consideration when making purchases. Not all of them will apply to every product category, but when they do, they can definitely help guide you in your decision. Look at the list below and decide which categories apply to you. Then, as you read through the second section, look for the lifestyle considerations to help you reach the best decision possible.

lifestyle considerations

Space. Whether you're short on it or have plenty to spare, space is a big consideration, especially when it comes to gear and furniture. Some people can afford to have all the bells and whistles because they have the space for it, while others need the most compact and minimalist choices in order to squeeze it all in.

Bells and whistles. If neither space nor budget is an issue, you might prefer your highchairs, strollers, and other equipment to come fully loaded with bonus features. These little extras can make your life easier, but they're purely optional: plenty of parents get by just fine without them.

Multistage. Even though multistage products may cost a little more up front, they can pay off in the long run. These products grow with your child and provide years of use; one smart buy could save you several independent purchases.

Portability. Parents on the go should look for products that are lightweight, compact, and, in some cases, collapsible. There are a lot of great choices out there for traveling tots; you just have to know what to look for.

Style. What's your personal style? Are you an antique lover looking for something traditional, or are you a design enthusiast who wants something more contemporary? Maybe you're a minimalist who wants low-profile items that will hardly be noticed.

Health. Of course all parents want the best for their baby, and health is an important consideration. Plus, we're all concerned about the state of the planet these days. There are a lot of smart choices you can make that will help cut down on the chemicals your child is exposed to, and we'll let you know what to look for in materials and fabrication.

Ready? Before long, you'll be an expert on baby products—and not because you have so many of them piled in your garage!

checklists
for expecting parents

if you're in that first blush of parenthood known as "expecting," the excitement has probably set in. In fact, many parents-to-be are so eager to get a jump on parenthood that they want to rush out and buy the whole baby store. But wait!

Once the word is out, you'll get lots of advice from your friends, family, and doctor (not to mention random strangers at the grocery store). Weigh your options carefully and consult baby guides to find out what you really need and want.

The next step is to create a baby registry. Sure, it's a handy way to let your friends and family know what you need and want—and anyone who's ever shopped for a baby gift can appreciate the wisdom in that. But it also helps you plan for your baby's arrival by keeping track of what's left to buy.

In the meantime, get used to the idea of being a parent and take a little time to bask in the glow of anticipation. Then, take a deep breath and get ready!

learning:
building your parenting library

Aren't you glad you don't have to do this alone? There's tons of advice out there on having a baby, raising a baby, shopping for your baby, teaching your baby. . . . And while your friends may be fonts of advice, you'll want to hear what the experts have to say, too. Use this time to hit the books and build your own crash course in Parenting 101.

pregnancy guide

First things first. You'll want a guide to help you wrap your head around this monumental event in your life and prepare you for the physiological and emotional changes that come with pregnancy. Good guides are part reality and part personal philosophy, and they come in a range of voices and outlooks. Look to your friends for recommendations, since they will probably have similar tastes.

gear guides

This book is a great start to give you an overview of what you'll need. The next step is a consumer guide that gives specifications and ratings for specific brands and products. A guide with peer reviews can be a big help in finding out what really works, since sorting through the facts and features can be a little overwhelming without the context of personal experience.

parenting guide

A lot of expecting parents worry whether they will know what to do when it comes time to be a parent. Luckily, there are plenty of guides out there offering expert advice on all sorts of parenting topics, such as child care or sleep training. Again, these are part expert information and part personal philosophy, so make sure you find the guide that's right for you.

health and safety books

A good, encyclopedic guide to children's health issues can be a lifesaver. Not only will it cover topics like how to take care of your baby and avoid emergencies, but it can also let you know what's normal and what's not, so you don't have to run to the doctor every time your baby sneezes. These guides can also be a huge help in teaching you how to describe symptoms over the phone.

play and activity guides

These how-to guides teach ways to encourage development through activities for children at every age. With older kids you can play catch, but what do you do with a three-month-old? You might also be able to find a regional guide that suggests fun local activities for children in your area.

post-partum perspectives

These books can help you understand your feelings during this time of hormonal upheaval and let you know you're not alone. They can also give you a context for your emotions, so you'll know what's normal and how long you'll feel that way. Many moms have friends or family they can talk to, but sometimes a book can help with issues you're not comfortable discussing. Few moms want to admit they're feeling resentment toward their precious six-month-old baby, but it happens.

journals and scrapbooks

There are journals for when you're expecting and scrapbooks to document your baby's first year—all sorts of options for documenting this exciting time. They can serve as a repository for all your thoughts, feelings, hopes, and dreams, not to mention all that memorabilia you're collecting.

early reading books

There's certainly not any hurry, but it's never too early to start collecting board books to read with your baby.

music

Choose something soothing to listen to during your pregnancy, including something soothing to listen to during labor. If you believe your baby can hear the music in utero, you might try to instill an early appreciation of Mozart. Then comes selecting music to listen to with your child. Whether it's classical, lullabies, or jazz, it's never too early to start exposing your child to good music.

pampering:
taking care of the mom-to-be

This is the time to embrace and nurture your changing body. The next couple of years will be all about taking care of the baby, but for now your job is to take care of you. Come to think of it, taking care of yourself is also good for the baby, so if you don't do it for yourself, do it for your future progeny. There are plenty of products designed to comfort and support you during your pregnancy, and you shouldn't hesitate to do whatever it takes to make yourself feel better. It's all about you—at least for the next few months.

stretch-mark remedy

Your body's changing, and so should your beauty routine—at least for now. Pamper your curves and growing belly with stretch-mark creams and oils. The verdict is out on whether they actually prevent stretch marks, but they certainly can't hurt. And in the meantime, they feel luxurious and keep your skin supple and moisturized.

leg cream

During pregnancy, your legs don't get as much circulation, and you're carrying a lot more water than normal, so pick up stimulating leg cream for swollen ankles and aching legs.

bath salts

Since you're carrying something new around with you 24/7, you're likely to experience soreness in your back, especially as the baby grows heavier. Take time to soothe and relax tired muscles with bath salts (but check with your doctor first).

back-rub oil

You'll never have a better excuse to ask for a back rub than when you're pregnant, so make sure you have some massage oil on hand. It's also an excellent excuse for a little couple time.

lightly fragranced products

You may experience a heightened sense of smell during pregnancy and want to go easy on the fragrances for a while. Whether it's bath products, lotions, or perfumes, look for mild, natural fragrances or fragrance-free products.

good maternity wear

Gone are the days of smocks, muumuus, and flowered tent dresses. Fortunately, designers have injected a lot more style into maternity wear—princess waistlines entirely optional.

support garments

Get a good maternity bra to bolster your burgeoning bosom. And if you're a runner, try a lower-back support belt. Plan ahead, so the moment you start to feel the changes, you're ready.

heart monitor

Be smart about exercise and listen to your doctor's advice. A heart monitor will help make sure you don't overdo things. Soon, you'll have to pull out the stroller just to go for a walk, so take advantage of this time of relative simplicity.

pregnancy vitamins

Every expecting mom needs pregnancy vitamins. Consult your doctors to find out what you need to keep you and your baby healthy and happy.

nesting: setting up your nursery

This is a time of nesting, and you'll want everything to be perfect when you bring your new baby home from the hospital. Beyond a few essentials, you don't actually have to have everything finished before the baby arrives (the baby won't know the difference). But the more you get done in advance, the more time you can spend staring at your bundle of joy instead of picking out curtains.

Another good reason to get things done early? To give fumes a chance to dissipate. So if you're going to paint, wallpaper, or put in new carpeting, do it a month or two in advance. (Or have someone *else* do it months in advance—you shouldn't be breathing the fumes either.)

Once you've got the foundation laid, it's time to start feathering your nest. Here are the building blocks of your baby's first bedroom.

a place to sleep

Whether it's a crib, a cradle, a bassinet, or a co-sleeper, you're going to need a place for the baby to sleep. See the crib section (page 108) to learn more about all of these options.

a mattress

Most cradles, bassinets, and co-sleepers come with their own mattress, but if not, you'll need to get one. Cribs rarely include a mattress, so make sure you remember to get one when you're picking out your crib. If you decide to buy a specialty or foreign-designed crib, keep in mind that it will require a different sized mattress.

bedding accessories

Most domestic crib mattresses come in a standard size and so will all of the bedding accessories, but again, specialty and foreign cribs will need accessories made to fit.

dust-mite barrier encasement

A must-have for protecting your child from allergens if you don't have an organic mattress.

mattress pad

Not only is this a waterproof barrier, it adds a nice layer of padding over a plastic-encased mattress.

fitted sheets

Just a note: babies don't sleep with a flat top sheet, which is why your baby's cute new crib set doesn't come with one.

baby blanket

For safety reasons, your child should only sleep with a breathable woven blanket. Comforters and quilts are purely decorative and should not be kept in the crib.

sleep sacks

As an alternative to a blanket, more and more parents are turning to sleep sacks—a kind of wearable, pajamalike blanket that is thought to help prevent SIDS and is made to be diaper-change friendly.

☐ changing table

While not essential, changing tables provide a dedicated supply station for diapering and a secure place for nervous new-parent hands.

☐ changing pad

If you have a changing table, you'll need a changing pad for safety and comfort. The sides of the pad should curve up on both sides to minimize rolling while your hands are busy with other important matters.

☐ changing-pad covers

You only need one changing pad, but you'll need a couple of covers so that you can swap them out when one needs to be washed.

changing-table essentials

Stock up on diapers, and make sure you have cleansing wipes, diaper cream or vitamin barrier cream, and a good diaper pail that closes securely. (Splurge a little on a good diaper pail—your nose will thank you.)

rocker or glider

While not essential, a softback rocker or glider with an extra-large seat is ideal for nursing and bedtime stories.

health aids

Make sure your baby-care kit has a digital thermometer, a basic first-aid kit, and nail clippers. Consult with your pediatrician to find out what else you should have on hand.

sensitive cleaning supplies

All parents want to keep their baby's nursery as clean and germ-free as possible, but keep in mind that there are toxins associated with cleaning products, too. Choose basic, non-toxic cleaners, surface wipes, and laundry detergent to make sure your baby doesn't suffer from cleaning overkill.

crib toys

Newborns can't sit up or hold anything and are just beginning to see movement, so toys at this stage should be simple. Best bets are a crib mobile and soft toys that hang from the crib, car seat, or stroller.

decor

Decorating is the icing on the cake: lamps, wall art, wall hangings—all for fun, and all up to you. Pick a color, pick a theme, or go eclectic. You'll be spending a lot of time in the nursery, so make it a place you and your baby can both appreciate. Remember—decor is the easiest element to change in a nursery, so don't take these decisions too seriously.

the big day:
coming home from the hospital

The good news is you don't have to have everything your baby will ever need before they're even born. Start out simple. Here's our list of everything you'll need before you bring your baby home from the hospital—sort of a Newborn Starter Kit. Anything else, you can worry about later, after you've gotten your feet back under you.

infant car seats

Your baby's first car seat is a big decision and an important must-have. Make sure you're prepared well before the big day, since they won't even let you take your baby home from the hospital without one (and wouldn't *that* be embarrassing?). Check out the car seat section for guidance on this important purchase (page 64).

co-sleeper, bassinet, or crib

You don't need to have made a final decision about sleeping arrangements the day your baby comes home from the hospital, but if you haven't arranged for some sort of bed, it's time to do so. (Even if *you're* not planning on sleeping those first few nights, your baby's going to want to.)

baby clothes

Stock up on sleeping gowns, onesies, hats, mits, and booties. Focus on comfort and practicality, and look for a chemical-free finish. This is an easy stage to find organic options that are cute and healthy.

diapers

The jury's still out on which is actually better for the environment—disposable or cloth. And most moms will argue over which is better for baby. Really, it comes down to personal preference. Don't invest in a lifetime supply until you've tried them both out and know which option you prefer. Even among disposable brands, you're likely to find you'll have a clear preference.

receiving blankets

These are the utility infielders of a nursery. Use them for swaddling, holding, warming, sleeping, changing, and playing. You'll want these right away, and you can never have too many.

burp cloths

You'll also want to have plenty of burp cloths around (or at least some extra cloth diapers). They're not only good for protecting your clothes from unexpected eruptions, they'll also protect your baby from snuzzling into dry-cleaning finish and other chemicals found in our clothes. They're also the first things you'll grab when there's an emergency cleanup situation.

nursing or feeding essentials

Whether you'll primarily breast-feed or bottle-feed, it will be good to have some supplies on hand for both, including breast pumps and bottles. See the feeding section (page 135) for more about picking the supplies that are right for you.

bathing accessories

With bath products, less is definitely more. Babies are delicate, and gentle skin care softens their introduction to our chemical world, so choose mild, hypoallergenic, antiallergenic, natural, or organic products.

diaper care

Daily use of a nontoxic barrier cream along with everyday wipes for sensitive skin is a great way to keep a diapered bottom rash-free. If a rash should occur, try to look for a more potent cream with echinacea.

checklists
for the first six months

for the first six months after your baby is born, a lot of your energy will revolve around the simple physical needs of the baby, such as nursing, diapering, and bathing. It's a fun and exciting time, and a lot of parents wonder if they're "doing it right." Relax. It's easier than it looks. And a lot of it just boils down to having the right tools to help you along and make your job easier.

These checklists will get you through the first six months. In the meantime, enjoy this wonderful time, filled with lots of fabulous firsts!

basics: tools for everyday living

You got your baby home from the hospital—now what? In addition to all the early must-haves, here are some of the things that will make your job easier during the first six months.

stroller

A stroller will help you get out and about and show your beautiful new baby off to the world. There are tons of options; look to our stroller section (page 78) for guidance on how to choose one.

carrier or sling

Most experts say nothing is more important to an infant's development than touch. That's why it's good to have a carrier or sling to keep baby close to you as you go about your day.

flexible sleeping

No matter what your original sleeping plan, be prepared to be flexible. Rather than jumping up every half hour to soothe a baby who can't seem to stay asleep, you might consider a bassinet or co-sleeper so you can bring baby into your bedroom.

swaddles

Some people believe that swaddling your baby mimics the feeling of being in the womb. Whether or not you subscribe to that belief, tight cuddling in a familiar blanket comforts many babies and helps them sleep—and who can argue with that?

sleep sacks

Sleep sacks are wearable blankets that keep your baby warm at night (and are even thought to help prevent SIDS). They also make great baby bedding on the go.

bouncy seat

A bouncy seat can make all the difference when you're trying to keep your baby amused for a few minutes so you can eat more than two bites in a row.

play mat

A play mat protects your child from the floor—and vice versa. During this early stage, it can also work as a bed on the go so your baby can catch a nap while you catch up with a friend over a cup of coffee.

nursery monitor

Monitors can be a new parent's best friend—giving you the confidence to step away from your sleeping baby for a book break in the other room, or perhaps even for your own snooze.

clothing: your baby basics

Most first-time parents have no idea whether they prefer T-shirts to bodysuits, pajamas to gowns, or plain undershirts to onesies that snap. The only way to find out is to try some of each. Your baby will probably have very clear likes and dislikes, as will you, so you'll want to collaborate on finding the best matches for you both. The best approach is not to buy too many of any given thing until you've explored all your options. (We've included starter quantities next to each.)

Remember, babies look cute in everything, so comfort is more important than looks. Stretchy materials will help ease the transitions from playtime to mealtime to naptime. And be sure to pay special attention to the fabrication. Look for formaldehyde-free finishes and avoid unnecessary chemicals that may irritate young skin.

bodysuits or onesies (4)

Tucking in tees over little rounded bellies is a never-ending task. But a bodysuit—like a T-shirt that snaps between the legs—will always stay in place.

footed bodysuits (2)

This no-fuss garment covers baby from neck to toe, combining a tee, pants, and booties into one piece. Great for both day and night!

tees (4)

Whether short-sleeved or long-sleeved, these are simply pint-size tees, but usually more fitted, like an undershirt. While they can be worn on their own, most are bought to go underneath outfits.

footed pants (2 pairs)

Keeping booties on little feet can be as tricky as keeping tees tucked in, but footed pants are a great solution.

baby gowns (2)

These make middle-of-the-night diaper changes a lot easier, since there are no zippers, snaps, or legs to navigate in the dark. They make daytime diaper changes easier, too, so don't think of them solely as a sleeping option.

booties (3 pairs)

Booties are like loose-fitting socks, with an elastic ankle band to help keep them on. Until your baby is walking, this is really all she'll need to wear on her feet.

mitts (3 pairs)

Made more for protection than climate control, mitts are like booties for the hands. Your baby's little fingernails may not feel dangerous to you, but they can scratch and mark his delicate skin.

caps (3)

Babies are bald, so they need all the help they can get. Caps keep little heads warm and can also act as a sun-shield. Fitted caps are a favorite for sleeping, especially if they have a little elastic.

cloth diapers (4)

Even if you've settled on disposable diapers, consider keeping at least one set of cloth diapers on hand. You can use them periodically to double-check urine flow, which is easier to judge with cloth than with disposable. And many parents claim they make the best burp cloths because they're compact and easy to wash. Whatever your diaper choice, your investment won't go to waste.

nursing: the original liquid diet

Whether you've chosen breast-feeding or bottle-feeding, the first six months are liquid only. Some children will start on soft cereals before six months, but the general rule of thumb is that you don't introduce solids until then. Consult your pediatrician to get the full scoop.

burp cloths

You can buy burp cloths or you can use spare cloth diapers; either way, you'll want to have plenty around. Look for soft, 100 percent cotton cloths, and maybe even buy organic, since your baby will be laying his or her face against it on a regular basis. They also make great cleanup cloths and cover a multitude of little uses.

nursing pillow

Everyone who nurses should have a breast-feeding support pillow. These rounded pillows fit around your waist and support your baby. Good ones have useful lives beyond breast-feeding support: they're perfect for helping support babies as they learn to sit up.

breast pump

Sad but true: you might not be able to spend every single moment at your baby's beck and call. For those times when you can't, you'll need a breast pump; see our breast pump section (page 140) for more information.

freezer trays or storage bags

If you want easy storage—especially if you need to store a lot of milk—freezer trays with lids or disposable storage bags are both great solutions.

nursing poncho

Whether you feel fearless or squeamish about breast-feeding in public, it's going to happen eventually. While you can always find some refuge under a receiving blanket, ponchos offer dependable privacy because they won't fall off.

bibs

There are smaller bibs for drool, as well as larger bibs that provide more coverage for feeding and such. Either way, they save load after load of laundry.

diapering: time for a change

During the early months, you could end up taking that trip to the changing table as many as eighteen times a day. Yikes! The good news is you won't find anything very offensive in baby's diapers until they're on solids. To help you prepare for doody-duty, make sure you've got everything you need to do the job right.

diapers

Cloth or disposable? There's no easy answer, except that it's your choice. You might want to look into one of the newer, smarter hybrids that are part cloth and part disposable. Our suggestion? Don't invest too heavily in either solution at the beginning.

baby wipes

Oh, the wipes you will go through! This is the baby equivalent of toilet paper, so be prepared.

diaper cream

Whether it's a daily protective barrier or an ointment for rashes, a good diaper cream will help keep your baby comfortable and happy.

changing table

Set up a changing area at home, whether it's a changing table or just a designated space with supplies nearby. Changing tables provide plenty of easy-to-organize storage space, but the end of the bed will also work if you put down a portable changing mat and take extra care to keep your baby from rolling.

diaper bag

Have your diaper bag set up and ready to go, stocked with every-thing you need for diapering away from home (see page 98). Portable changing pads are almost standard in diaper bags now, but burp cloths and blankets can usually serve in a pinch.

diaper pails

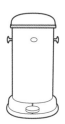

You don't technically have to have a diaper pail, as you can put disposables in the trash and cloth diapers into the laundry. But most people prefer a quick and easy place to hide the evidence. Spend a little extra to seal in the smell, and remember: no plas-tic pails are truly airtight. Also, be aware that some diaper pails need special diaper-pail bags, while others can take any regular garbage bag.

bathing: get ready for tub-time

A lot of parents find bath-time to be among their favorite parent-ing activities. It's a great time for bonding, and there's nothing like a giggling, splashing child to lift your spirits. As with most things, babies need their own set of supplies for the bath, but the general rule for bathing products is that less is more. Here's what you'll need.

infant tub or bath seat

Both are simple and inexpensive plastic devices that hold your child in a safe, comfortable position while you bathe him. To get the full scoop, see the tub section (page 164).

hooded towels

A cross between a towel and a robe, these provide head-to-toe coverage for your little one straight out of the bath, and some even have fun animal heads.

natural sponge or soft washcloth

At the beginning, a little warm water and a sponge or cloth go a long way. We recommend soft, natural sponges because they're small enough to get even the little parts clean.

baby spa care

Stick with the basics. A gentle cleanser that works as both shampoo and body wash is really all you'll need in the beginning. Everything else can be added as conditions arise.

tub toys

Bath-time can turn into one of your favorite activities with the help of bath squirters, floating animals, bubbles, and other toys.

teething: soothing secrets

There's no getting around it: every baby teethes—and teething hurts. Toys will end up in your baby's mouth from the beginning, but when they start gnawing on them, and there's a ton of drool, that's a good sign it's time for a teether. This is a short list, but it's critical for curing crankiness.

cloth teethers

If your baby's going to chew on his or her toys anyway, you might as well get some that are made to go in the mouth. These are small, soft toys your child can chew on to soothe sore gums.

freezable teethers

When teething really starts to get painful, try a teether that can go in the freezer. These are usually made of plastic and filled with a freezable liquid; the ice helps numb the pain.

medicinal supplies

Consult your pediatrician to find out what products she recommends to help ease your baby's discomfort. There are also a number of herbal remedies available on the market if you're interested in natural solutions.

drool bibs

Teething means drooling, and drooling means laundry. Invest in some drool bibs to save your child's clothing.

checklists
for toddlerhood

so you've made it through the first several months, and you're ready to start thinking about next steps. Speaking of steps, your baby will be taking his or her first before you know it, then it'll be on to walking and running. Be ready to get your exercise the good, old-fashioned way: trying to keep up with your toddler. Your baby will be growing, moving, and enjoying a whole new range of activities, which means a whole new stage of purchases.

growing:
bigger baby, different stuff

Soon, your child will be on the move and growing in earnest. Which means you'll be trading in your stroller bassinet seat, portable car seat, and front carrier, and making a whole new round of purchases to accommodate your growing child.

☐ toddler car seat

Unless you bought a convertible car seat that transitions from infant to toddler, you'll need to upgrade to a larger toddler car seat, which means you won't be able to pop it in and out of the car like you could with the infant seat.

☐ backpacks

At some point, your child will outgrow his front carrier—or get too big for you to be able to carry him in one comfortably. Once your child has adequate head and neck control—usually after one year—you can start using a backpack. And yes, that means there will be a few months in between where neither solution is appropriate. Check out some of the new hybrid hip carriers designed to get you through the gap.

☐ umbrella stroller

Eventually, the benefits of having a lightweight stroller will start to outweigh having all the bells and whistles. An umbrella-style stroller (so called because it folds up like an umbrella) is your most lightweight and portable option, perfect for travel and quick trips, when you don't want to mess with a full-size stroller.

personal care

Say good-bye to that sweet, new-baby smell and say hello to a new approach to personal care. Simple soap and water will be replaced with kid shampoos and soaps—and don't forget the bubble bath! You'll know it's time to reassess your current bathroom supplies when your baby starts smelling like a *kid*.

toddler tub

If you've managed to get away with sink baths so far, lucky you! At six months, it's time to graduate your child from a reclining position to a seated position, which means transitioning to a toddler tub or bath seat that sits inside your regular bathtub.

real shoes

Babies have chubby little feet that start out more rounded than flat, so resist hard soles and patent leather and look for shoes that are flexible, soft, and simple. As your baby becomes a full-blown walker, you'll move to shoes with a little more structure and sole protection.

toddler toys

As your baby gets stronger and more coordinated, look for toys that enhance motor skills. Balls that can be thrown but won't roll too far encourage repetition and mastery. As language starts to emerge, music, books, and activities that encourage verbal and audial development will be a big hit. As your child becomes a toddler, add interactive and role-playing toys, like puppets, building blocks, tool sets, dollhouses, train sets, and kitchens.

eating: introducing real food

Somewhere around the magical six-month mark, you'll begin the transition into solid foods. Though entertaining at times, this stage can also be time-consuming and messy. There's a whole new range of products you'll need to make it through mealtime, many of which will make your job a whole lot easier.

cookbooks

Baby cookbooks provide plenty of help, and the best ones break it down into the basics. As your child gets older, look for books that let you cook one meal for the whole family.

food mill

No matter which cookbook you follow, everything is mashed in the first phase of baby food. A food mill is one of the most useful and least expensive items you can own. You can buy a big electronic one, but a good, hand-held food mill will do the trick for most parents, and it will be a kitchen staple for years to come.

high chair

What kind of high chair you'll want will depend on your lifestyle, the age of your baby, and how much space you have to store the chair. Check out our high chair section (page 147) for guidance.

bibs

Bibs are made to catch mealtime messes, so make sure you choose ones that are easy to clean—maybe even with a pocket to catch dribbled food.

bib clips

These handy devices consist of a cord with two clips that let you make your own bib out of just about anything—from a paper towel to a cloth diaper to a dish towel. This is a good option for parents on the go who want to travel with less, or even parents on a budget who want to be resourceful.

spoons

When you first introduce baby food, you'll want a soft spoon that's easy on the gums, with a long handle for airplane-style food delivery. At around one year, babies start wanting to help themselves; you can encourage their learning with soft, short spoons that make scooping easy.

toddler utensils

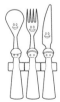

Once your child has mastered her own spoon, she'll soon be ready for forks and, eventually, even knives. Toddler utensils should be smaller than mom-and-dad utensils, with soft, easy-to-grasp handles.

sippy cups

These lidded cups with a small spout for drinking will save your carpets from being covered in big juicy splotches and are essential for taking your toddler's drinks "to go."

splash mats

A splash mat can save your wood floors and dining room rugs—not to mention your back! Instead of having to clean dropped food off the floor, you just lift the mat and shake it out or wash it.

food-storage containers

You'll need sealable containers for the refrigerator, but you might also want to invest in some food trays for the freezer. Like an ice tray with a lid, these trays offer single-serving storage and are stackable and space-efficient.

to-go containers

In addition to food-storage containers, you'll want containers to keep in your diaper bag for snacking on the go. Make sure you choose something that minimizes spills while allowing your baby easy access to what she needs.

toothbrush

Now that your baby is eating, he needs to start brushing. It's important for gum health as well as teeth, so you'll want to start even before all his teeth are in. Start with a small, kid-size brush; then, as he gets older, move to a simple electronic brush for maximum self-help. This is especially important once your child hits birthday party age, when cake and ice cream consumption make brushing really critical.

potty training: graduating diapers

Imagine a world without diapers. Ahhhhh. The good news is that the day *will* come when you'll no longer have to do diaper duty. The bad news: you'll have to go through potty training to get there. It can be challenging, but the right tools make a big difference.

Avoid potty seats that are overly complicated or awkward to use, or that kids might have difficulty getting on and off of. Remember, if it looks difficult to use, it probably is. Whatever you get, make sure it's sturdy and stable. Nothing will hamper toilet training like a seat your child is afraid they're going to fall off of.

potty seat

Start with a simple, sturdy potty seat that's independent from the toilet (ones that attach to the toilet are often too advanced for beginners).

toilet-seat trainer

When your child is ready to take on the real toilet, a toilet trainer helps smooth the way by making the hole in the seat smaller so there's no fear of falling in.

step stool

This is an essential accessory for the grown-up toilet, until your child is big enough to climb up unassisted.

portable trainer

When you're traveling, these provide a sanitary seat for a little one who doesn't get the idea of a public restroom.

training pants

From disposable options to regular cloth, there are styles for every preference as you transition your child out of diapers. Night trainers will be your new best friends as your child learns to get through the night without incident.

easy-on and -off clothing

Avoid unintentional barriers to success. In other words, now is not the time for buttons and belts. Look for loose-fitting pants with elastic waistbands that are easier to get on and off.

educational support

Kid-friendly books that introduce your child to the notion of potty training will help open up a dialogue and ease the transition out of diapers.

safety-proofing:
getting the house ready

When your child starts moving around, it's time to safety-proof *everything*. Some people safety-proof before the baby comes, but you might want to consider whether to bother with the inconvenience before you really have to. The bottom line is, when your child becomes mobile, you'll need to be ready so she can develop a healthy curiosity and still remain safe. The first step is removing any items that can break or be eaten; then you can incorporate some of the following as needed.

smoke and carbon monoxide detectors

These detectors should be installed before the baby arrives. If you don't have them yet, make it a top priority—for your own safety as well as your child's. If you have them installed already, make sure they still work and have fresh batteries.

outlet plugs or covers

These are fairly low-hassle and a must-have for any home with a child. Make sure you have one for every outlet in the house.

corner and edge protectors

You don't need to cover every corner and hard edge, but if you have any that are really scary—such as glass or metal—these protectors can save you a trip to the emergency room.

cabinet locks

Evaluate the contents of cabinets that are accessible to your toddler, and get locks for ones you don't want her exploring. This is especially important for medicine cabinets and cabinets with cleaners and other toxic substances.

toilet latch

This isn't just about keeping toys from getting flushed; toilets actually pose a drowning risk. So even though they might be a pain, you'll probably want to get these latches installed.

blind-winders

The strings hanging off of blinds are a hazard to crawling and walking toddlers. To avoid a dangerous tangle, blind-winders keep the cords neatly out of reach.

baby gates

Not everyone needs these. But if you have stairs, gates are a must for preventing action movie–style tumbles. Gates can also be used to restrict access to more dangerous rooms, such as offices with lots of cords.

specialty items specific to your house

There are many types of safety-proofing tools that can help with any specific needs your house presents. These include window guards for high-rise buildings, door-jams for swinging doors that could pinch fingers, and oven-dial protectors for front-facing stove dials.

checklists
for getting out and about

whether your child is three weeks old or three years old,
you'll need a whole new set of equipment for getting out of the
house. You can't take along everything you own—though you'll
probably be tempted to try. With a few essentials, you'll be prepared for getting out and about with baby, whether it's on a family
vacation or just your daily outings.

traveling:
arriving with your sanity intact

Just because you have the kids in tow, there's no need to stress: a little bit of planning can go a long way toward reducing travel headaches. If you're traveling by air, don't kick off your trip with a fussy flier; pick a time when your child is most likely to be asleep. Book a flight that coincides with nap-time, or, for longer distances, consider taking a red-eye. In the meantime, consider having the following on hand for anything from a family vacation to a weekend at Grandma's.

travel-friendly stroller

Make sure you have a stroller that won't drive you crazy—especially when navigating airports. For advice, see our section on strollers (page 78).

baby carrier

Consider wearing a front carrier or sling to transport the newest member of your family through the airport. These carriers make it easy to get on and off the plane, and for those of you who'll fly with your baby in your lap, they provide a comfortable, hands-free place to let baby sleep and nurse.

food storage

Whether it's sippy cups, bowls with tops, or small containers with openings that will only release a couple of raisins at a time, sturdy food-storage containers are a traveling mom's best friend.

moist wipes

These come in handy pocket packs and are great for all sorts of little cleanups. Regular diaper wipes can work for spills, or you can bring along face wipes that are appropriate for baby's sensitive skin.

clothing

Choose comfy clothes for you and your baby so that you can both rest easy during travel. Layers are key, both for adjusting to changes in temperature and keeping your child looking cute and tidy. Just peel off (or throw on) a layer and, voilà! No one has to know what your child's been eating for the last several hours.

activities

Bored kids are restless kids, so bring along plenty of interactive activities to keep them occupied. The best choices don't have a lot of pieces to drop or throw and come in their own storage container for easy pack-up. Make sure the toys are quiet and won't disturb the other passengers.

diaper wallet

The diaper-bag version of a regular wallet, this holds just the essentials—diapers, wipes, and a changing surface—and can be tied on to a stroller or piece of luggage so you have one less bag to carry.

portable potty seat

Public bathrooms can be scary, but a portable potty seat makes a nice, clean layer between your child and the rest of the world. (Make sure you have a plastic bag to store it in along the way.)

travel bed

When traveling with an infant, consider these two shortcuts to a portable crib: For parents who co-sleep, portable co-sleepers make sleeping on the road as comfortable and easy as at home. For those who don't, try one of the new travel cots that fit in your suitcase and don't need to be checked as another bag.

favorite blanket

For practical and transitional reasons, pack a familiar blankie for naps and nighttime. Most hotels offer only adult-size blankets. Not only are they too heavy to cover a small baby with, they won't smell a bit like home.

baby monitor

These are often overlooked while packing, but when your baby is napping and you're downstairs enjoying a glass of wine with the family, you'll be glad you brought it along.

☐ travel health kit

Having a sick baby when you're away from home is no fun for anyone, but being prepared can help save you some stress. Be sure you have a thermometer and a bottle of temperature-control medicine for emergencies.

☐ toiletries

Face wipes are great for travel touch-ups, and two-in-one and no-rinse washes help keep things simple. Look for travel kits with pint-size versions of your favorite products.

☐ outlet plugs or covers

Hotel rooms and guest bedrooms are seldom baby-proofed. Bring your own outlet covers from home for one less thing to worry about on the road.

outdoors: fun in the sun

Even if you're not hanging out at the beach, your child will spend more time in the sun when you're outdoors than you realize. Whether it's a trip in the stroller or "just one more minute" on the swing set, that sun exposure can really add up. Children's skin is more delicate than adults', and more susceptible to damage from the sun's harmful rays, so don't leave the house without these sun-care essentials.

sunscreen

Be sure to apply sunscreen to exposed skin, even for a quick afternoon stroll. See our discussion on page 171 to find out more about choosing the most effective one.

hats and sunglasses

Sunglasses and hats add another layer of defense against sun damage. Start children early to get them used to the idea, and take advantage of sun hats with chin ties for as long as you can get away with it. (Often, toddlers who don't wear them early on will decide that they just don't "do" hats.)

protective coverage

As skin cancer continues to raise our awareness of the importance of UV protection, more parents are choosing bodysuits over swimsuits for extra coverage at the pool. And for other summer-time outings, you might want to consider UV-protectant clothes, like lightweight pants and tunic tops.

umbrella

Even if your child has sunscreen on, an umbrella is an easy way to provide a physical barrier to UV rays—especially at peak hours. Many strollers and backpacks come with their own umbrellas, but if yours didn't, it's easy to find one you can add on.

weather:
getting out in the snow and rain

Even trickier than preparing for a sunny day outing is preparing for one in inclement weather. While no product can replace the need for common sense in assessing whether you should just stay in where it's warm and dry, some products can be a life-saver for the outdoor adventurer with baby in tow.

winter bunting

One zip and your child is covered by this full-body parka that covers everything but eyes, nose, and mouth.

mittens

Keep little fingers well protected, since they get less blood flow, to keep them warm, than other body parts.

hats

A good percentage of body heat escapes through the scalp, so make sure your baby's little bald head is protected on chilly days.

booties

For outdoor use, look for heavier booties made with wind-resistant exterior materials for the cold.

rain or weather shields

A rain or weather shield for your car seat or stroller can make all the difference when trekking outdoors with your baby in bad weather. The weather shield is usually only necessary in extremely cold climates, but a rain shield is a must-have for the unexpected downpour.

cold cream

The only thing you can't cover up in cold weather is your baby's face. But you can protect his delicate skin with cold cream, which helps soothe and prevent the chapping caused by strong wind or extreme cold.

sunscreen and sunglasses

Don't be fooled by cold or rain—the sun can still reach you and your baby through the clouds! You should protect whatever skin is exposed, just like you would at the beach.

products
for baby on the go

babies are simpler than adults in a lot of ways, but one area where they need extra attention is getting out in the world. To take ourselves for a walk, we just have to throw on a pair of shoes. A baby needs a car seat for car trips, a stroller or carrier for foot trips, and a diaper bag for every trip. You might look back wistfully on the days when you didn't have to pack a bag just to leave the house, but at least you can make it as painless as possible, with the right products.

.............car seats....................................

As far as the law is concerned, diapers, clothes, and a bed for your baby are all optional. A car seat is the only item you're legally required to buy—no ifs, ands, or buts. It doesn't even matter if you don't have a car; most hospitals take it so seriously that they won't let you take your child home until you have a car seat, even if you just carry your child in it as you walk home on foot.

So there's no question whether you're getting one; the question is just what kind and how many. We might as well go ahead and break it to you, you'll probably end up having to buy three separate car seats to cover three different sizes of child: an infant seat, a toddler seat, and a booster seat. The only exceptions are if you buy a convertible car seat that covers two stages, allowing you to buy just two seats, or if you have a newer-model car that comes with its own booster seat, thus cutting out one of the purchases.

This is one of the few categories that the experts unanimously recommend not taking a hand-me-down to save some expense. Car seat technology is always changing, and since it's a safety issue, you'll want the most up-to-date style available.

The sheer quantity of seats to choose from can be intimidating, but you can narrow the field pretty quickly if you have an idea of what you're looking for. So buckle up—you're about to learn everything you ever needed to know about car seats!

your basic choices

There are four basic types of car seat, and the difference between them has to do with what size your child is. We'll go into more detail in the stage considerations section (see page 70), but here are the basic differences.

infant seat

Your infant car seat is designed for approximately the first six to nine months. The primary feature of infant car seats is that they're portable, thanks to their detachable base, which means you can get sleeping babies in and out of the car without waking them. These seats are designed for rear-facing installation only. Yes, this means the child will be in the backseat facing away from you, which can be hard, but it's much safer (and it's the law).

toddler seat

This is the car seat you'll need from around six months of age up to four years, or about 40 pounds, whichever comes first. The American Academy of Pediatrics recommends keeping car seats rear-facing until your baby reaches one year of age. After that, these car seats can be installed facing forward.

booster seat

The booster seat is for kids who are too big for a toddler seat but too small to be released from car-seatdom altogether. They get to use the car's seat-belt system just like the grown-ups; the booster seat just provides a little extra protection—and a little bit of a height boost. State laws vary on how long you must keep your child in a booster seat, but the seats are designed to be used from the ages of four to eight years and from 30 to 100 pounds.

products for baby on the go

[CAR SEATS]

convertible

Remember how we said you might be able to get away with just two car seats? The key would be to buy a convertible car seat that covers two of the three stages. There are two types: one that combines the infant seat and toddler seat, and one that combines the toddler seat and booster seat. They still haven't found a way to make one seat that can work from infancy up to eight years (and would we really want them to?).

general guidance

All the different combinations might start to make your head spin (or is that just morning sickness?), so here's a quick synopsis of your options.

infant seat, toddler seat, and booster seat. By buying all three seats separately, you get the best features of each stage, but it does end up costing a little more.

infant/toddler convertible plus booster seat. This combination saves money since you're only buying two seats, but you lose the portability of a dedicated infant seat.

infant seat plus toddler/booster convertible. This combination also saves money since you're only buying two seats, but there's a space trade-off since a toddler/booster convertible is typically a lot bigger than a booster seat.

The good news is, you only need to make one choice to start with, and that's whether to buy an infant seat or an infant/toddler convertible seat.

Parents who will take the baby in the car only occasionally might opt for the convertible seat rather than an infant seat. Here's why: the infant-seat stage only lasts around six or seven months—nine tops. This means that if you don't drive much, you'll only enjoy the portability of the infant seat a handful of times—which probably won't be worth the extra expense. But parents who are in and out of the car all the time will probably prefer to spend the money on a standard infant seat.

car safety standards

All child car seats sold in the United States must be designed to meet a safety standard set by the federal government in 1981, so you never have to worry whether a car seat being sold in a store is "up to code." But there are a lot of other ratings that could help you decide just how far beyond the basic requirements a car seat manufacturer has gone.

- The NHTSA (National Highway Traffic Safety Administration) does an annual Ease of Use rating.

- The JPMA (Juvenile Products Manufacturers' Association) has developed a unique certification program that has been guiding parents for more than 25 years. The JPMA Certification Seal on a product or its package ensures the product was built to the very highest safety standards.

- The ASTM (American Society for Testing and Materials), a highly regarded nonprofit organization, publishes the voluntary standards used in the JPMA Certification Program. Industry members work together with the U.S. Consumer Product Safety Commission, consumer groups, and other interested parties to develop the standards.

- Consumer Reports is the only organization in the United States to rate car seats for crash protection (though they don't do it every year).

See Resources (page 176) for more details.

Whatever you decide, a car seat is one purchase you shouldn't skimp on. Your primary consideration should be the car seat's safety ratings; then you can factor in ease of installation, ease of use, cost, and style to make your final decision. The car you drive will also impact your decision. If you have a newer car with a high safety rating, you don't need to worry quite as much, but if you have an older model, you'll want the biggest, safest car seat money can buy.

Car seats today come in a range of fabric and textile choices. Don't be swayed by nice upholstery before you've checked up on the safety features. And if your favorite car seat comes in an atrocious pea green or a tacky pattern that you just can't bear, you can always disguise it with a pretty car seat cover, which manufacturers have started to make in a variety of colors, patterns, and materials.

to LATCH or not to LATCH?

In September of 2002, U.S. government regulations mandated that new cars and car seats must be manufactured with the LATCH system (Lower Anchors and Tethers for Children).

The LATCH system lets you attach your car seat to sturdy upper and lower anchors that are built into your car—a faster, safer, and easier alternative to using the seat-belts to buckle in the car seat. The result is a more solid connection between car and car seat, giving you more stability in the event of a crash.

If you have a car with the LATCH system, you'll want a LATCH car seat to match. If you have an older car that doesn't have the LATCH system, this feature won't be as important. However, if you think you might change cars at any point, you might want to get the LATCH car seat anyway. You can still attach it to your old car using seat-belts, and you'll be glad to have it if you upgrade cars.

features to look for

good safety rating. Every seat on the market meets the minimum safety standards, but you'll want the safest car seat you can find, especially if you have an older car. Generally, more expensive models are more expensive because of their extra attention to safety features like head cushioning and side-impact protection.

easy installation. If your car is LATCH-equipped, you won't have to worry as much about ease of installation, since LATCH systems work the same in most cars. But if your car isn't LATCH-equipped, make sure your car seat is easy to install with confidence.

five-point harness. These secure your child in place at the shoulders, at the hips, and between the legs for maximum security and come standard in every car seat. If you do use a hand-me-down seat, make sure it has this important safety feature.

front harness adjusters. Adjusting a harness in the back is like doing it with your eyes closed, so make sure you can adjust it from the front—especially considering you'll have to do it every time you put the baby in the car.

level indicator. This mechanism—which varies by model— is a gauge that eases your stress level at initial installation by letting you know whether or not you've installed your car seat properly.

adjustable sun canopy. This is a simple device that protects your child from the sun's glare, no matter which direction it's coming from.

removable/washable fabric and pads. Unless you bought the car seat just to spring your baby from the maternity ward, it's going to get dirty, so look for removable and washable pads and upholstery.

stage considerations

first stage: infant car seat

You've already read about all the features you should look for in a car seat, but here are some guidelines that are specific to the infant car seat.

 • **Separate car seat base.** This is one of the key features of an infant car seat and what makes it portable. You install the base, have your local fire or police department review your installation, and then never have to worry about it again. From there, you just click the seat in and out of the base.

a tip for two-car families

If you're a two-car family, and the child will travel in one car most of the time, you might want to buy both an infant seat *and* an infant/toddler convertible at the beginning to save yourself the expense of having to buy an extra infant car seat base to install in the second car.

Here's how it works: Install the infant seat in the primary car your child will travel in, so you can still enjoy the portability of the infant seat most of the time. Install the infant/toddler convertible seat in the second car, the one that's not used as often. That way, there's a car seat ready and waiting in that car—one that you would have to buy eventually anyway. With the money you saved by not buying a second infant car seat base (which isn't cheap), you can afford to buy an even better infant/toddler seat.

• **Weight.** One of the big advantages of the infant car seat is that it's smaller and more portable. To take advantage of this portability, make sure the one you select is light enough for you to carry.

• **Stroller compatibility.** To take convenience and portability one step further, you might want to consider an infant car seat that's compatible with your stroller, or even get a universal system (see page 79 of stroller section). Instead of trying to transfer your sleeping baby to a stroller without waking her up—good luck with that—you can just pop the car seat into the stroller base and be on your way!

• **Cushioning.** In the beginning, your newborn will seem tiny and fragile in a car seat. Whether you buy a seat with lots of padding or buy separate inserts, you'll definitely want some padding, so factor it into your pricing up front.

• **Adjustable recline option.** This feature allows you to recline the seat, making it easier for your child to sleep in the car. (No more lolling heads!)

second stage: toddler seat

You already know what to look for in a car seat (and you can refresh your memory in the first part of this chapter if you haven't read it since you were picking your infant seat). Once you've checked off everything you want from that list, factor in these considerations that are particular to toddler car seats.

Remember, this is the car seat your child will spend the most years in, so don't try to cut corners—you'll want the best!

• **Size.** Some toddler seats are huge. Before you purchase, be sure to test your top choice in your car to make sure it fits, especially if you have multiple car seats or a really small car.

• **Safety rating.** Safety ratings in second-stage car seats cover a lot more variables, so keep your particular car in mind when making your choice. Consider your car's roll-over and side-impact ratings and discuss these factors with your retailer. If you drive an economy car, it makes more sense to spend more on your car seat than if you drive a top-of-the-line, safety-rated vehicle.

• **Convertibility.** If you plan on having more than one child, you may want to consider buying a seat that converts from a toddler seat to a booster seat at this point. There are a lot of great options, and this choice will help minimize your parent-hood product-accumulation problem.

• **Cushioning.** Make sure your toddler has plenty of padding and that the seat is comfortable, especially since this is the seat your child will use the longest. Cushioning and head support in the car seat will encourage naps—always welcome with a toddler—and help prevent drooping heads.

third stage: booster seat

These seats are made to accommodate children up to eight years old and 100 pounds, but check your local laws; children may be able to graduate out of their boosters sooner than that. As a general rule, however, once your child's ears extend above the back of the booster seat, or if his shoulders reach the top harness slots, he's ready to use the car's regular seat-belt system.

• **Seat-belt adjusters.** Make sure your booster seat includes seat-belt adjusters. This will help you avoid the unnecessary frustration of twisted or tangled seat-belts and ensure that the seat-belt is at the right position for your child's changing height.

• **Booster back.** Boosters come in two forms: one with a back and one without. Both use the car's seat-belt system and give the child added height. What style is right for you depends on your car, your child's age and size, and how many car seats you need to fit in your back seat. As a rule of thumb, children below 40 pounds need a booster with a back. After that, it's a matter of personal preference (and state law—so check yours).

• **Convertibility.** If you bought a toddler seat that converts into a booster, you'll configure it like a toddler seat until the child is about 40 pounds. After 40 pounds, simply remove the five-point harness and use the car's own seat-belt system until the child outgrows the need for a booster.

convertible/multistage

In general, you'll want to look for the same features in a convertible seat that you would with the two regular car seats it will replace.

But the bigger question is whether a convertible car seat is right for you. We'll let you in on a little secret here: most people eventually end up buying all three seats. But a convertible seat remains a great choice for certain families. It really depends on your lifestyle.

A convertible car seat that covers both the infant and toddler stages saves you money, but you'll be sacrificing the portability of the infant seat. This might be a good option, however, if you don't drive very often.

With a convertible seat that covers the toddler and booster stages, you'll sacrifice backseat space as your child gets older, since toddler seats can be a lot bigger than booster seats. For families trying to fit multiple car seats in their car, it's worth buying a separate booster seat. Another issue is that, as your child gets bigger, they might resist getting in and out of the more cumbersome convertible.

lifestyle considerations

space. Since toddler car seats seldom make it into the house, you only have to worry about whether it will fit in your car. Before you buy, try it out in your backseat—especially if you're going to have more than one car seat. Unless you have a particularly large child, you can get a smaller seat by giving up some of the bells and whistles.

multistage. A convertible car seat saves you a purchase by allowing you to buy two car seats instead of three.

portability. There's no getting around the fact that later-stage car seats are inherently unwieldy and inconvenient to travel with, but you can ease the burden with a wheeled or backpack-style car seat carrier. In general, look for a smaller and lighter car seat or booster with a high safety rating, and make sure you can carry it.

usage tips

• Follow the manufacturer's instructions for installation; if your car seat moves more than one inch in any direction, it's not installed correctly. All experts agree that the key to car seat safety is proper installation.

• Don't be shy about asking for help installing your car seat. If you don't have an experienced friend you can ask, call the National Highway Traffic Safety Administration or your local police or fire department.

• Car seats should always be installed in the backseat. The exceptions are pickups and two-seaters, in which case the front seat is your only choice, and minivans or other vehicles with three rows of seats, in which case the middle row is the safest.

• For safety purposes, never use a car seat in a seat equipped with air bags. The force with which they deploy is too strong. If your only option is a seat with an air bag, you'll need to have the air bag disabled; if you don't know how to do this, ask your mechanic.

• The carry handle on an infant car seat usually swings from an upright position for carrying into a downward position when in the car. Remember to place the handle in the vehicle position before each trip.

• The American Academy of Pediatrics recommends keeping your car seat rear-facing until your child reaches one year of age and at least 30 pounds.

products for baby on the go

[CAR SEATS]

• Adjust your seat straps at the right height. In general, straps should be snug. For rear-facing seats, the shoulder straps should be at shoulder height or slightly lower. For front-facing seats, the shoulder straps should be slightly above the shoulders. If you can slide one finger between the baby and the strap, you've got it in just right.

• Send in your manufacturer's registration card to ensure that you're notified of any recalls.

• If you have a LATCH system, use it. But never install a car seat using both the LATCH strap and the vehicle safety belt. This restricts the belts from absorbing crash energy and lowers their crash safety ratings. If you don't have the LATCH system, just be sure to follow your safety installation instructions.

accessories

car seat insert for newborns. A newborn can look awfully small and vulnerable in a car seat, but a padded insert can keep your baby extra snug. Many car seats come with more than enough padding, though, so wait until you've made your car seat purchase.

car seat blanket. These special blankets stay in place much better than a standard blanket because they work with the car seat's harness and zip up around the child. The blanket will keep your little one warm and cozy during car trips, and you can easily zip the top part off without removing your child from the seat.

car seat cover. Love the seat but hate the fabric? Or has your beautiful car seat suffered one too many juice incidents? A spiffy new car seat cover can add new life—and style—for a lot less money than buying a replacement.

extra infant car seat bases. If you have more than one car, go wild! Equip each vehicle the baby rides in with its own car seat base. Then you never have to worry about reinstalling the base, and you can just click the seat in and out.

car seat carrier. If you're taking your car seat on a plane, you might want a carrier that allows you to carry it more easily, while also protecting the upholstery from the perils of travel. Some have backpack straps and others even have wheels.

seat protector. Consider buying this accessory to protect your vehicle's seat from the wear and tear of having a car seat in place—especially if you have leather seats. Some car seats can't be installed correctly with a seat protector under them, but most can. Save your receipt just in case.

window sunshade. Sun protection is an important consideration for cars without tinted windows and car seats without canopies. Even in a car with tinted windows, the direct sun can be uncomfortably warm.

pacifier strap. The worst part about the rear-facing car seat is listening to your baby cry and knowing there's nothing you can do about it short of pulling over. One of the leading culprits of an upset baby is a dropped binky. Get a strap that hooks onto the car seat to help prevent this midtrip meltdown.

products for baby on the go

strollers.

There's no rule saying you have to have a stroller, but it's hard to imagine not having one if you're ever planning to leave the house. And as your child starts to feel more and more like a large and wiggly sack of potatoes, you'll really appreciate the extra mobility.

This is one of your bigger-ticket items, so you'll want to make sure you pick the right one. And there are a lot more choices on the market than there used to be in terms of style, price, and function. In the past, you just picked the upholstery you liked best and made sure it rolled in a forward direction. Nowadays, buying a stroller is more like buying a high-performance bicycle or other piece of equipment—which is why more dads get involved in stroller purchases than any other category of baby products.

Most parents end up buying two strollers: one for primary use and one to fulfill whatever needs the first one doesn't. For example, you might get a full-size stroller and then add a lightweight, collapsible one. Or you might want to add a jogger that can't be used every day, but will let you get out and get some exercise.

More and more stroller models are trying to be all things to all people—the one that does it all. This means that the different categories of stroller have started to overlap. The problem is, by trying to do it all, they don't do their original job quite as well. A lightweight, collapsible stroller might add fully reclining seats so that it can be used in the infant stage, but suddenly it's not as lightweight or collapsible anymore.

Sound complicated? Well, it is. But once you have an under-standing of the different types, their benefits, and how they match up to your needs as a parent, you can really start to home in on what you want.

your basic choices

full-size strollers

These are the larger, sturdier, and more expensive strollers, also referred to as standard strollers, prams, or carriages. Most have a bassinet stage, allowing the baby to lie flat, as well as a reclining seat for when the child is old enough to sit. Usually fully loaded, these strollers are all about adapt-ability and the child's comfort.

umbrella strollers

These folding strollers are called umbrella strollers for their curved, umbrella-like handles and easy, single-handed fold-ing. They're the best option for a high-quality, lightweight, durable stroller that's ideal for hopping in and out of cars, traveling, or navigating small spaces. The umbrella stroller is most parents' must-have second stroller—and for most, it's the preferred choice for the toddler stage.

universal systems

A universal stroller system is a collapsible, four-wheeled frame that you can click your infant car seat into—more like a wheeled accessory for your car seat rather than a true stroller. This option is called a universal system because it's made to work with any infant car seat. While relatively inexpensive, you may not need one of these if your full-size stroller comes with universal functionality.

travel systems

Similar to the universal system, travel systems have a universal frame that can hold a car seat. But travel systems also come with a simple toddler seat that will work as a lightweight stroller until the child is around four years old. Sometimes referred to as "convenience strollers," they're also similar to an umbrella stroller, although often not quite as lightweight or durable.

all-terrain strollers

These are the sport-utility vehicles of the stroller world, and a great alternative to buying both a full-size stroller and a separate jogger. Typically, these have all the features of a full-size stroller, including a bassinet stage, and they also offer easier maneuvering, durability, and lightweight, full-suspension wheels. Most include a universal functionality that lets you use them with your infant car seat.

joggers

These three-wheeled strollers are aerodynamically designed for the serious runner. Made for either trail or street running, they're relatively lightweight and include a hand brake and a safety strap for the parent's wrist. They tend to be a bit less maneuverable in small spaces than an all-terrain, as a trade-off to their more aerodynamic design.

doubles and triples

You can only push one stroller at a time—but what if you have more than one child? For twins, or if you have more than one stroller-aged child, a double stroller is a good solution. One style is a side-by-side stroller, which is good for togetherness but bad for fitting through the checkout line at the store. The other style is an in-line stroller that places one child in front of the other. Both are available in a lightweight umbrella style or a sturdier full-size style. If you have triplets, you can even get a three-seater.

general guidance

Most couples end up with at least two strollers, no matter what they think they'll buy at the beginning. We'll give you plenty of advice for picking a model later, but first you'll need to figure out what *kind* of stroller you want.

for your primary stroller:

• If you mostly travel by car (rather than having to navigate public tranportation) and want more cargo space for your bags and your child's things, you'll likely prefer a full-size, fully loaded stroller as your primary stroller.

• If you want all the bells and whistles of a full-size stroller but are an active parent who likes to be outdoors a lot, and if you normally use your car to get around (rather than public transportation), you'll get the highest value and fit with an all-terrain stroller for your primary stroller.

• If you're going to be taking public transportation a lot and need portability, or if you're a minimalist who would prefer to carry your child as much as possible, you may be able to get away with just an umbrella stroller, which you can start using a few months into parenthood (check models for minimum requirements). Few parents can do this, however, and most who do still end up getting a universal system as backup for use with their car seat, particularly if they live in a suburban area.

for your secondary stroller:

• Almost all parents who have a full-size or all-terrain stroller also end up buying an umbrella stroller. For some, this is a must-have travel companion, and for others, it offers ease and flexibility for quick jaunts especially during the toddler stage. Some parents end up ditching their full-size altogether and using this as their main stroller from about two years old on.

• No matter what their primary stroller choice, serious runners will typically also invest in a jogger. Increasingly, joggers are more and more like regular strollers, offering things like adapters for infant car seats. However, the more features like this they offer, the less likely they are ideal for the serious jogger.

• Travel systems are purchased mostly by frequent travelers, although with the greater durability of umbrella strollers—not to mention the option of renting a car seat along with your rental car—many busy travelers are quite satisfied with umbrella strollers for most of their needs and don't invest in an entire travel setup.

• Double strollers often become a second stroller for parents with more than one child. Most still prefer the single-stroller option for one-on-one time, but need the two-kid setup for single-parent outings with multiple kids.

other factors to consider

Now that you've thought about what kind of stroller you want, you can start to focus on what you should look for. Here are some questions you should ask yourself before you get started.

• Are you a city dweller who has to navigate curbs, rough surfaces, and public transportation? Think small and lightweight, but durable.

• Are you a suburban parent who drives most places and only uses the stroller on smooth, paved surfaces? You have room for a lot more stroller, but you'll still need to be able to lift it in and out of a car easily.

• Are there lots of stairs in your daily life? Don't forget that you'll probably be climbing the stairs with a stroller in one hand and your baby in the other, so factor weight and collapsibility into your purchase decision.

For the most part, you'll find there's a trade-off between a stroller's size and weight and its durability. If you live in the city and want something that's easy to get around with, you may want a stroller that's smaller, leaner, and easier to handle—even if you might have to replace it in a year. However, if you don't have to navigate stairs and storage isn't an issue you might want a bigger, sturdier stroller that can take a lot more abuse and will last for more than one child.

Any stroller you buy will take some training, but make sure you're able to collapse, adjust, and maneuver it with ease before committing to the purchase. It might take some instruction, as well as some trial and error, but if you still find it hard to handle after a few tries, you should search out a model that's easier for you. You'll be opening, closing, and steering your stroller with one hand—often when you're in a hurry or juggling too much in a crowded place—so it's important to make it easy on yourself.

features to look for

car seat compatibility. If you're going to spend a lot on a full-size or all-terrain stroller, look for one that's compatible with your car seat, especially if you'll be in and out of your car a lot.

adjustable handlebars. Handlebar-height adjustability can be among the more important features for comfortable use over time, particularly for parents with very different heights.

type of handlebar. While most full-size strollers have one straight handlebar, most umbrella strollers have two curved handles (much like umbrellas). The straight handlebar makes navigating a little easier, but the two curved bars make the stroller more collapsible, so consider the trade-off.

legroom (yours!). Spend some time testing how comfortable you are striding behind different strollers, and make sure you have a good fit. The size of the wheels, angle of the seat, and handlebar positions all affect the legroom for the parent.

expandability. Some strollers offer multibaby or multistage options that will allow you to keep adding to your growing family with your first investment.

durability. With any luck, you might be able to use your stroller for more than one child. Be sure to consider wheel construction, as some wheel types can begin to stick and become difficult to maneuver over time.

washability. Make sure you consider the stickiness factor and get a stroller that's easy to clean.

cargo space. Just about every stroller comes with a storage basket, though the size and style can vary almost as much as the strollers themselves. Decide if you're a pack rat or a minimalist, and choose your stroller accordingly.

seat reversibility. Many full-size and all-terrain strollers give you the choice of which direction to face the baby. You'll probably want to start out with your baby facing you, which can make all the difference between feeling like you spent time with your baby rather than just pushing a stroller.

brakes. This safety feature keeps your stroller from rolling away when you're not moving. Look for brakes that are conveniently located, for when your hands are full. If you live in a hilly city, you might also want resistance brakes that will slow your stroller down on an incline.

locking front wheels. Normally, wheels are made to rotate from side to side independently for maximum maneuverability. But many four-wheel, all-terrain strollers will have front wheels that lock off so that they roll together, allowing it to operate more like a jogger and making it easier to go in a straight line.

adjustable seat position. In most full-size and all-terrain strollers, the seat will have multiple positions so that your child can sit straight up, recline slightly, or stretch out for a nap while you walk.

jogger features. If you're buying a jogger, you should consider collapsibility, overall weight, size and style of the wheels, and the availability of replacement parts and service.

safety strap. All strollers come with a strap, located near the handlebars, so you can attach it around your wrist for extra security. No more runaway prams! As crazy as it sounds, it can happen.

stage considerations

More and more, you can find one stroller to accommodate different stages, rather than having to buy different strollers at different ages. In general, strollers will work for up to around 40 pounds or four years. Joggers tend to be used longer—up to 50 pounds, on average.

• As a general rule, a stroller is only appropriate for a newborn if it has a fully reclined position, whether it's a bassinet or a seat that reclines all the way. You'll use your stroller in the fully reclined position for the first six months of your baby's life. After that, your child will be in the toddler seat (taking advantage of the different levels of recline) until he or she outgrows strollers altogether.

• There are more deluxe models of umbrella strollers that fully recline and offer enough head support for infants, but in all cases, you should check the recommended age profile for each stroller.

• Some joggers now offer a full-recline or bassinet stage, but it is generally not recommended to use the stroller for high-impact activity or jogging until the baby is at least six months old.

• Strollers should not be used on uneven surfaces during the first six months in the bassinet stage. That's why all-terrain strollers typically have a feature to lock out the suspension in the first stage—to keep the stroller from bouncing as it absorbs shock.

• Most double strollers have seats that recline individually, meaning one baby can lie back while the other sits up. This is key when you have children at different ages.

lifestyle considerations

space. If you live in an apartment and don't have a garage, you'll really appreciate having a small umbrella stroller that can be folded up and put in a corner. For the early stages (before an umbrella can be used), a travel or universal system is best.

bells and whistles. If you like lots of features, the standard full-size or all-terrain stroller might be for you. The trade-off is in price and portability.

multistage. Most full-size and all-terrain strollers come equipped with the settings and accessories you need to get you all the way through your child's stroller career. All-terrain strollers also have a multifunction benefit, in that they can save you from having to buy a separate jogger.

portability. You have a lot of options when it comes to travel. You can get a universal system that lets you attach your car seat to wheels, a travel system, or an easily folded umbrella stroller. Some people prefer a travel system, but they're not really necessary if you already have a stroller with universal functionality. Our best tip? Get a lightweight umbrella stroller. After the first six months, it's the easiest to travel with.

style. It's understandable to want the coolest-looking stroller, since you'll be seen out and about with it. But remember, in the long run, it's really about your lifestyle, so make sure you're not choosing form over function.

usage tips

• Always use the harness system. When your baby gets older, it's tempting to let her sit in the seat without the belt on, but trust us, you don't want to learn your lesson the hard way (such as suffering a spill coming off a street corner).

• Be careful hanging diaper bags, grocery bags, purses, backpacks, and other items off the back of your stroller; an overloaded stroller can tip, remember, small babies don't weigh that much.

• Strollers are for sitting or lying down. Don't let your child stand in the stroller for any reason.

• Make sure your stroller is fully open before putting baby in. Partially collapsed strollers can not only scare your baby but also pinch a hand or leg. Whether you're opening or closing the stroller, do it completely and without baby in or around the activity.

• Be careful on hills. Just like bicycles, strollers can gain speed. Busy parents with busy hands should use extra caution going down hills, particularly on hills that descend into intersections. This might be a good time to put on that safety strap!

• Just like regular oil checks for your car, periodic mainte-nance for strollers is a good idea. This is especially true as strollers have become fancier, offer more options, and are built more like high-tech bicycles than old-style prams. Air-filled tires mean tires that can go flat. (Too bad there aren't oil and lube shops for strollers.)

accessories

rain cover. This is a must-have in case you get caught in a rainstorm. These covers are included with most full-size and all-terrain strollers, but if not, you can get a universal cover that will work with any of them.

sunshade or canopy. If you walk outside a lot, an adjustable sun-shield is a good way to protect your baby from the sun—especially if she loves to play the pull-the-hat-off game.

mosquito netting. Few people actually use this, but depending on where you live, this may be important to you. You also might consider it if you like to camp. Most full-size and all-terrain strollers come with this optional accessory.

infant head support. Depending on the amount of cushioning your stroller comes with, you might want to get a cushioned insert to hold your child's head in place—particularly when your baby is young.

cup and food holders. Your stroller might come equipped with these or offer them as an option, but if not, it's easy to add on universal holders that work with any stroller.

bag clips. These are great for hanging groceries from your stroller handlebars. They may come with your stroller or need to be purchased separately. (Just be careful not to overload the stroller.)

stroller blanket. Though a standard crib blanket will do, many strollers include fitted foot muffs or "boots" for snuggly cruising, especially for the bassinet stage. You can also find stroller blankets that hook on to the stroller and work with the harness. Both options are great because they're impossible to kick off.

stroller travel bag. If you'll be traveling with your stroller, you might want a bag designed to carry it in. But wait until you've gone on your first trip before making the investment— you'll know a lot more about your parent travel style at that time and be able to make a more informed choice.

stroller hanging toys. Whether it's a toy with a Velcro closure for hanging from a crib or something you can attach with a strap, it's nice to have something your child can play with but not lose.

car-seat adapter. If you buy a stroller with car-seat capability, you'll more than likely need an adapter that works with the frame. These are seldom included in the initial purchase, though some fully loaded stroller options don't require an adapter at all.

wheeled boards. Have an older child who's past the stroller stage but every once in a while needs a lift? Wheeled boards allow an older sibling to ride along on the back of the younger sibling's stroller. Few kids use them regularly, and they can be awkward, but they're a fun addition for some families.

......baby carriers...................................

You'd think after being carried in someone's stomach for nine months, a baby would want a little alone time, but far from it! Human contact is not only reassuring, but also necessary for proper development. In fact, developmental experts say that nothing is more important for an infant than touch.

But you have a life to live. You can't sit around holding the baby every minute of the day, even as much as you might want to.

Enter baby carriers.

Whatever its form, a baby carrier helps do the heavy lifting, so to speak, and allows you to keep your child close by. And a good hands-free option will even free you up to go about many of your everyday tasks.

When you're out and about, a stroller is certainly an option, but the carrier is a great choice to sustain the parent-child connection. It can be especially nice for dads, who didn't get the "benefit" of carrying their child inside them for nine months. And sometimes it's just easier than having to deal with a stroller.

Even when your child starts to walk, there will certainly be plenty of times they're going to look at you with those big eyes and issue some version of the command, "Up! Up!" A carrier will not only make this task easier (or, if you're petite, *possible*), it will distribute the weight better and keep you from killing your back.

your basic choices

For the early months, your choices are either a traditional front carrier or a sling, and that decision largely boils down to personal preference. Kids outgrow front carriers within the first year, and most will outgrow their slings, as well. Then you either move into the territory of hybrids and backpacks or start relying on your stroller more.

traditional front carriers

These popular carriers hold the baby in a seated position against your chest. Because they're designed for hands-free use, they allow you to keep your baby close while you clean the house, shop, or walk. They can be used just a few weeks after the baby is born with the baby positioned facing the parent.

slings

A sling is a fabric carrier that lets you carry your baby in front of you in a hammock position. Slings require a little more awareness but are a great choice for nursing mothers. They come in two styles: the more traditional kind, made of a single piece of fabric in sizes made to fit the parent, or the updated, one-size-fits-all sling with adjustable straps.

new hybrids and hip holders

The newer multi-position carriers cover that age when your child is too big for a sling or carrier, but not big enough for a backpack. Most parents do a lot of hip carrying, which not only ties up your hands, it's hard on your back. A hip carrier can make all the difference. You might find you even prefer it to a backpack. Some hip carriers evolve from a front carrier or sling, and some are made just for hip use.

backpacks

Backpacks are a second-stage carrying solution for when your child has outgrown the other carriers. Pediatricians don't recommend using them before one year, or until your child has developed adequate head and neck control. Most backpacks have support frames that distribute the weight properly and help ease the strain on parents' backs.

general guidance

Whether to choose a sling or traditional carrier is a personal preference, and one that's hard to predict. Traditional carriers are typically the pick of North American parents, while slings are more popular in Europe. Slings have, however, been gaining popularity in urban centers of the United States. Here are some of the factors to consider when making your choice.

hands-free use. The big advantage of a carrier is that it lets you keep your baby close to you while keeping your hands free, so you can go about your day. It also allows you to do what you need to do (for the most part) knowing the baby is securely fastened; a sling always requires more awareness because there aren't safety straps to hold your baby in.

nursing. For nursing mothers, the sling offers the easiest, quickest, and most discreet access.

your comfort. Parents who prefer carriers often argue that unless a sling fits you just right, it can hit you at a level that's uncomfortable. Also, most carriers come with back support and shoulder support (more like a good backpack), making them easier for the parent to carry, especially as the baby grows.

your baby's comfort. A sling allows your baby to lie at your waist in a comfortable sleeping position and even leverages the natural swing motion of your walking. Plus, the material wraps the baby with a similar nesting effect to swaddling.

longevity. The sling can have a longer useful life than the front carrier because you can also use it to support your toddler in the hip-carrying position.

The decision still mostly comes down to personal preference and what you feel more comfortable carrying. Our recommendation? Try a friend's before you buy.

Some mothers enjoy having one of each: a sling for nursing early on and a carrier for extra support during more active times.

features to look for

size and adjustability. If more than one person will be sharing it, make sure you get a carrier that can easily adjust to fit either person. It's important that the sling or carrier fits well, and also that you don't have to spend a lot of time adjusting it.

machine-washable. No matter what kind of carrier you choose, it's going to get dirty if you use it more than just occasionally. Easy washability is a lifesaver.

storage pockets. In a traditional carrier or backpack, smart storage pockets might just save you from having to lug along a diaper bag, too.

back support. This isn't such an issue with newborns, but every month your baby grows, and so does your load. Make sure you pick a carrier that will provide you the back support you need, and definitely test before you buy, especially with traditional carriers and backpacks.

backpack features. When evaluating a backpack, consider what its headrest options are (for the inevitable sleeping toddler), whether it provides sun protection, and how easy it is to adjust for your child (not to mention mom and dad!). Bonus features are storage pouches, bottle packs, and loops for securing toys and pacifiers.

collapsibility. If you're transitioning into a backpack, you'll want to consider one that works like a normal backpack but opens up to expose a cushioned seat for your toddler. If you're mountain hiking with your child, you'll want a traditional backpack, but a collapsible backpack is ideal for the parent who wants to encourage her toddler to walk.

price. You get what you pay for. For the most part, what you pay more for is the addition of lumbar support and better shoulder pads. If you're going to be a heavy user, pay a little more for the one that will serve you best.

stage considerations

When deciding what type of carrier to use, keep in mind your baby's development as well as your own body. Two important considerations are your child's weight and whether he can hold his head up; also take into account your own size, strength, and how much back support you need.

• Slings may be used within the first couple of weeks, or as soon as you're ready to be out and about. Front carriers may be used for infants as early as the first couple of weeks of life, as long as there is adequate head support and the baby is facing the parent. When your child is strong enough to hold his or her head up, you can turn him facing out to see the world while you walk.

• Whether you choose a sling or front carrier, your child will likely outgrow it within the first year. The sling can enjoy extra life as a support for hip carrying; in other words, you can use the sling under your child's bottom to help distribute weight.

• Backpacks may be used as soon as the child has developed adequate head and neck control. Many pediatricians don't recommend using a backpack before one year.

• A hybrid hip carrier can bridge the gap between carriers and the backpack stage. For some parents, the hybrid does more than just bridge the gap: it's used as an everyday solution for hip carrying well into the toddler stage.

lifestyle considerations

bells and whistles. Some slings take a simpler, more natural approach, with just a single piece of fabric comprising the whole thing. But if you want more features, like pockets and clips, look for the next-generation, nylon slings or a more traditional carrier.

multistage. Technically, the most transitional/multistage option is a sling: you can go from the newborn position to using the sling like a hybrid to help hold the baby on your hip.

style. Some people think one-piece fabric slings have too much of a hippie, Earth Mother feel. If that's a problem for you, look for one of the more modern nylon slings that have an urban-gear kind of look. As for carriers, at least they come in black!

usage tips

• Carriers shouldn't be used while driving, jogging, skating, or riding a bicycle.

• Exercise caution when bending to pick something up while carrying a baby. Use your hand to hold baby in place, and bend at the knees rather than at the waist.

• Don't cook with a baby on your front in a carrier.

• Be careful when reaching for things that could fall on your baby.

• Pay attention to age, weight, and stage requirements for different styles of carriers.

• If you get a sarong-style sling, some coaching at the beginning can be very helpful in getting the fit right.

accessories

carrier covers. These simple covers are like blankets that hook onto the carrier so they won't fall off when you're out and about.

pacifier clips. Dropped binkies can be a sad fact of life, but these clips make sure they don't get left behind.

hats and sun covers. If you're carrying your child in a carrier, there's a good chance you'll end up outdoors, so be sure to protect your child from the sun's harmful rays.

diaper bags.

There are people who, before giving birth, would never in a million years think, "I'd like to carry a great big bag with *duckies* all over it!" And yet, when it comes time to choose a diaper bag, they'll choose a pastel bag with a cartoony pattern, which they tolerate at best.

If you really, really want a diaper bag in a duck motif, then more power to you. But don't choose the pattern for your kid—they're not the ones who have to carry it. Choose something that reflects your personal style. There are so many diaper bags to choose from, there's no good reason not to have a bag you really love to carry.

Diaper bags these days come in plenty of cool, contemporary styles that are specially designed for your convenience. Most include an insulated bottle holder, an easy-access changing pad compartment, and probably even the changing pad itself—not to mention little hooks to secure binkies and smaller items. Some even include an exterior opening for diaper wipes so that you can access them without opening your bag. All of these features help make it possible to maneuver around the bag with one hand, even while you're holding a sleeping child.

If you really want to express your style, you might consider a bag that wasn't specifically designed to be a diaper bag. Really, you can turn any bag into a diaper bag if it has a roomy interior compartment and good pockets—especially if you add in diaper-bag accessories, such as an insulated bottle holder.

your basic choices

The differences between diaper-bag options boil down to size and style. Almost all of your choices fall into one of the following five categories.

tote

This is the most common style of diaper bag and includes either one long shoulder strap or two shorter handle straps. The simplest version is just a tote bag with one big open compartment; a higher-end version would have more pockets and organizational capacity. Whether it's your primary diaper bag or a backup bag for the car, totes are one of the most popular styles for new parents.

messenger bag

A favorite with dads and city dwellers, messenger bags are a great way to stash baby's stuff in a way that will never be noticed. Usually designed with one long strap that can be worn over one shoulder or across the chest, they're a great hands-free option, and the most unisex of the bunch.

backpack

A great choice for comfort and hands-free use. The two straps help distribute the weight more evenly and are a great choice if you're going to be carrying a lot of stuff. You can convert a regular backpack into a diaper bag, since it will probably have lots of pockets anyway, but a good diaper backpack will serve you well with built-in features like a thermal bottle holder.

fashion bag

Fashion-conscious parents will want to keep their options open. This category covers all shapes, sizes, and materials, from luxurious leather to beautiful silk brocades. There's an astounding range of options, plus many major-name handbag manufacturers are getting in on the game.

the well-stocked diaper bag

Must have:

- spare diapers
- diaper wipes
- diaper cream
- changing pad or extra blanket
- change of clothes or spare onesie (just in case)
- a bottle or nursing supplies
- burp cloth (you can also use a spare cloth diaper)
- hat (for changes in weather or sun protection)

Nice to have:

- plastic bag to stash dirty diapers
- receiving blanket (fills in where needed)
- booties, hat, and mittens
- toys or books for an emergency distraction
- a pacifier, if you choose

Add after first six months:

- extra clothes (in case of accidents or spills)
- snacks and a sippy cup or bottle
- bib
- blanket (for any unplanned circumstances)
- disposable place mats
- antiseptic wipes and adhesive bandages

The key is finding a bag that's big enough to hold all your stuff. (Baby? What baby?)

sling
Like a more streamlined version of a backpack, the sling is worn over the shoulder and across the chest with a single strap. It distributes the weight more evenly and remains close to your chest so that you're not just lugging around a heavy bag hanging from a strap.

general guidance
to share or not to share? If you're going for personal style, you and your partner might want to have separate diaper bags. But the upside to sharing is that you only have to stock it once, and you never have to wonder who has the binky. If you do decide to share, you'll want to find a nice, neutral bag that everyone can agree on—which means avoiding that pattern you think is "so cute" and letting your husband have veto power over bubblegum pink.

comfort is key. Pick a bag that will be comfortable for you even when you're loaded up like a pack mule. The two things to look for are cushioning and adjustability, especially if you're going to be sharing with someone who's a different height. Make sure the bag will fit over your shoulder if you want to stay hands-free—and you *will* want to stay hands-free. Straps should have proper cushioning so they don't dig into your shoulders.

one great bag or lots of bags to choose from? Some people like to have one good, basic diaper bag, while others consider them an accessory and want to have several to choose from, just like their handbags.

easy cleanup. If you want a diaper bag that will stick with you through thick and thin, in sickness and in health, through juice spills and spit-ups, then you'll want one that's easy to clean. Messes happen. Avoid bags that can't get wet or dirty, and look for bags that are either washable or wipe clean easily.

seasonal considerations. One of the drawbacks of those great bags that just wipe clean is that many are made from plastic or pleather. While they're exceptionally easy to maintain, you might want to take climate into consideration, because they're made of materials that stay chilly in the winter and can be uncomfortably hot to carry in the summer.

personality. Babies can be just as different from each other as adults: some make a ton of messes, others don't seem to. Don't overbuy before you get to know your child's personality. After you have a little experience under your belt, you'll know what kind of bag works best.

parents of twins. Whether you're a minimalist or like to be prepared, having multiples means some of your supplies must multiply, too, so plan on a bigger bag. If you have a double-wide stroller, you can even get a double-wide bag made to fit the handlebars.

special-needs children. Parents of babies with special needs often find they have more to carry along; if this applies to you, plan on buying a bigger bag.

features to look for

changing pad. Most diaper bags come with a changing pad. If you're buying a bag that doesn't have one, make sure there's an opening big enough to store one in, because you'll definitely need a clean, comfortable surface to do your changing.

cargo space. If you're a pack rat and want everything with you all the time, you'll want a sturdy, high-capacity diaper bag. If you're a minimalist who wants to carry just the necessities, you'll want light, airy, and efficient. Many first-time parents want to be prepared for anything, but most will opt for the less-is-more route as their baby becomes a toddler.

easy (and quiet) access. Avoid complicated latches. When you're holding a fussy baby in one hand and fishing around in a diaper bag with the other hand, you'll appreciate the importance of easy access. A common misconception is that Velcro closures are the ultimate solution. While they are awfully handy, they can also wake up a sleeping baby—and neither of you will like that much. Look for magnetic or other quiet-closure solutions for your easy-access compartments.

insulated bottle holder. Many diaper bags come with one, but if yours doesn't, or you've chosen a nontraditional diaper bag, you can buy one separately to make sure your bag is properly equipped. Either way, you'll want one of these to keep your baby's bottle at the right temperature.

stroller compatibility. Make sure you have at least one good bag that works with your stroller. It doesn't have to match, but it should fit over your stroller handle, or at least in the storage bin, so you don't need three hands to walk the baby.

diaper wallet. These are essentially mini–diaper bags, made to carry just the essentials for quick trips out; some are sold as a set with a larger diaper bag. You'll appreciate the ease of grabbing a smaller load when you're just running to the store.

cell-phone compartment. Not a necessity, but a lot of parents find this feature handy—and you probably have a good idea whether or not you're one of those parents.

lifestyle considerations

space. Consider having a larger bag plus a diaper-bag wallet so you can plan according to how long you'll be out and about.

style. The diaper bag is one of the most prominent style choices you can make as a parent. It's the one piece of baby equipment that goes with you everywhere you go. Again, you're the one who has to carry it—not the baby—so make sure it's something you're comfortable to be seen with.

health. The one health consideration pertaining to diaper bags is more about you than the baby. Basically, you want a bag that won't strain your back. Make sure you have good padding on the straps and that the weight is distributed evenly. Think backpack if you're worried about ergonomics.

usage tips

• What you prefer in handbags will bear a lot of resemblance to what you'll like in diaper bags. Do you tend to overpack or travel light? Do you have one great bag or lots of bags to mix and match with your outfits?

• Plan for the fact that you won't need to carry as much as your baby grows from infant to toddler. Also, remember: when you have a newborn, you're usually carrying the baby and the bag; when you have a toddler, you're usually carrying the bag and chasing the child.

• If you have a diaper bag designed to hang over the stroller's handlebars, just make sure you don't load it up so much that you accidentally tip the stroller.

notes

products
for the nursery

few preparations are as exciting for new parents as putting together their baby's nursery. There are paint swatches to compare and curtains to be hung, maybe even a crucial choice to be made between a cloud motif or a day-at-the-zoo theme. You and your baby will be spending a lot of time together in the nursery, so of course you want everything to be perfect. And that doesn't just mean beautiful, but also comfortable and safe.

Don't sweat the decor too much because that's one of the easiest and most fun things to change. Focus your efforts on the big purchases first, then add the little touches that will make it the perfect place to bring your child home from the hospital.

cribs and beds

It's estimated that babies spend as much as eighteen hours a day in their crib during their first year, which means that you and the crib are pretty much going to be your baby's whole world. You'll want a bed that fits your style, but you'll also want something comfortable and safe.

Whether your baby goes straight to a crib or spends a few months in a bassinet, cradle, or co-sleeper is up to you. Most children end up in a crib eventually, though, so if you only want to buy one piece of furniture, that's the one. There are also great multistage options that take you from a bassinet to a crib to a toddler bed with just one purchase.

Cribs come in a lot of different styles, with all sorts of materials and finishes to choose from, so whatever look you're going for, it's easier than ever to find something you love.

Whatever style of bed you choose, avoid using hand-me-downs. Newer models are safer because safety standards have evolved, and older cribs might have rails that are farther apart than is considered safe.

your basic choices

Here are your choices for sleepy-time success.

cribs

The crib is the staple of the nursery, the one piece of furniture that everything else is designed around. Prices can range anywhere from $100 up to thousands for a custom crib. A crib that converts to a toddler bed can be well worth the investment because it adds another two to four years of use to your purchase.

bassinets and cradles

A smaller bed for your baby's first months—either a bassinet or a cradle that rocks—can add a nice, romantic touch to the nursery, though it's not a necessity by any means. One big upside is that they're small enough to move around the house, which means your baby can nap in any room (including your bedroom, making nighttime feedings more convenient).

co-sleepers

If you want to keep your child in the same bed as you, a co-sleeper is a small bed that either lies on top of your bed or attaches to the side of it, with sturdy sides to keep you from rolling over onto your infant while you sleep. The on-top-of-the-bed style can also double as a portable crib for parents on the go.

portable cribs

Portable cribs can be a lifesaver for frequent travelers, and they're also a good option for the grandparents' houses. Some fold and unfold and can also be used as everyday playpens. Newer options work more like pop-up tents, and while they don't double as playpens, they're smaller and more portable and double as a UV-protected tent for outdoors.

general guidance

cradles, bassinets, and co-sleepers. The important thing to know about these three types of beds is that they're all entirely optional. They do have a certain romantic appeal and take up less space, but in just three to six months, your child will need something bigger. (As a particular note for cradles, make sure that the rocking motion is easy to trigger and stays quiet!) None of these comes in a standard size, so if it doesn't include a mattress, make sure you can find one that fits.

portable cribs. When shopping for a portable crib, make sure it's lightweight enough to suit your needs, easy to set up and take down, easy to clean and care for, and durable enough to stand up to use. An included travel case, bag, or at least a handle is a simple, must-have feature to ensure portability.

mattresses. Just like with your own bed, you're going to want a good mattress to put in the crib. Almost all cribs use standard-size U.S. crib mattresses, and the general rule is that firmer is better. In fact, some studies have linked softer mattresses to SIDS (see sidebar, page 118, for more information about SIDS).

the risks and rewards of co-sleeping

Sharing a bed with your infant—or co-sleeping—is controversial in the United States. Supporters believe that a parent's bed is just where an infant belongs; opponents believe it's unsafe.

The benefits of co-sleeping? It encourages breast-feeding, makes it easier to get the baby to sleep, provides better sleep for both mom and baby, and encourages bonding, especially for working parents who don't get to see their child during the day.

The arguments against co-sleeping are mostly safety related. The big one is the danger of suffocation if a parent inadvertently rolls over onto the baby. But there are also concerns about the baby falling asleep facedown on a softer bed or getting stuck between the mattress and the headboard, wall, or nightstand. Some of these concerns can be mitigated with the use of a co-sleeper, which goes on top of your bed and has rigid walls, creating a smaller space that's safer for your child.

Talk to your pediatrician if you want a professional opinion, but where your child sleeps—whether it's in your bed or a crib—is a personal decision.

There are two basic types of mattress: foam and inner-spring. A good foam mattress is heavier and, when pushed on, bounces back quickly. An innerspring mattress should have a coil count of at least 150 and should be firm in the center as well as the edges.

Crib mattresses are typically covered with a quilted or laminated vinyl to enhance durability and water resistance. The exceptions are organic mattresses, which include wool mattresses with an innerspring construction and latex mattresses that are more like foam. If you choose an organic mattress, keep in mind that they don't have the vinyl covering, so be sure to pick up a waterproof mattress pad to protect your investment.

features to look for

crib rails. Cribs have two types of rails to choose from: fixed rails or drop rails. Fixed-rail cribs are generally sturdier, but drop rails can be lowered to make it easier to get baby in and out. Just be sure to test drop-rail cribs before buying to make sure the sides are easy to adjust.

convertibility. Today, most cribs convert into at least a toddler bed, and some also cover the bassinet stage, as well.

adjustable mattress height. All cribs have three or four mattress-height settings. The idea is to keep the mattress higher at first so it's easier to reach into the crib, then lower the mattress as your baby becomes more mobile to keep him from jumping or climbing out. Make sure it doesn't require a degree in crib design to change the mattress settings—you'll do it up to three times for each child!

under-crib drawers. Some manufacturers offer these as an option, and they can be a great storage solution for a crowded nursery. If your crib doesn't come with built-in drawers, you can always buy storage boxes or baskets to put below.

breathability. Make sure your crib, bassinet, or co-sleeper has a breathable construction and enough room for your child. This not only minimizes sweaty heads and improves sleep but is also a SIDS consideration.

stage considerations

• Cradles, bassinets, and co-sleepers are really only options for newborns and infants. Depending on the size of both your baby and the bed, these options will be useful only for three to six months.

• Cribs can be used from day one, and most children stay in a crib until sometime after their second birthday. A telltale sign your baby is about to outgrow his crib is when he starts trying to climb out.

• Cribs that convert into toddler beds can be used for five years or more, depending on the size of the child. These beds use the same mattress as the crib and include a protective bar to keep the sleeping child from falling out of bed.

• Portable cribs may be used for sleeping on the road for as long as you keep your child in a crib. Once your child has outgrown her crib—and is still learning to sleep without falling out of bed—you'll have to find a new solution when traveling, like an attachable guardrail or the old pillows-on-the-floor trick.

lifestyle considerations

portability. If you travel a lot, you'll want a portable crib; how often you travel will determine what kind. A portable crib that doubles as a playpen counts as another bag to check, while the pop-up-tent style is smaller and lighter and can be carried in your suitcase.

multistage. Be sure to take your family plans into consideration when choosing a crib. If you only have one child, you might get the most value out of a crib that converts to a toddler bed. If you're planning for more kids, though, you'll get plenty of use out of your nonconvertible crib.

usage tips

• Remove all pillows, stuffed animals, duvets, quilts, big blankets, and even teethers when baby is asleep or unattended.

• If you have a drop-rail crib, always remember to keep the side pulled up and locked in place when your baby is in the crib.

• Crib mattresses should fit snugly. The rule of thumb is no more than two adult fingers should be able to fit between the crib and mattress.

• On a regular basis, check your crib for any loose screws, bolts, brackets, chipped or peeling paint, splinters, or broken edges.

• Keep your crib safely out of reach of dangling cords, lamp shades, heaters, and anything else that might pose a risk.

• Make sure there's enough breathing room in your cradle, bassinet, or co-sleeper that your baby won't get overheated.

• Portable cribs should not be used on a permanent basis; they don't have the durability for safe long-term use.

accessories

canopy or bonnet. Purely decorative, but these add a sweet touch to cradles and bassinets.

crib mobiles. Developmentally speaking, bold black-and-white graphics are a great choice for newborns. Just be sure the mobile is not hanging low enough for your child to grab once he starts standing.

sound machines. Some people opt for sound machines that attach to the outside of the crib and include soothing music or nature sounds.

nursery linens

You'd think making up your baby's bed would be approximately the same as making your own. But there are differences, from the things you add to the things you take away.

Probably the biggest difference is what you won't use on your baby's bed. No top sheets, no quilts, no pillows. And don't let that beautiful comforter and pillow sham sold with your crib set fool you; they should only be used for decorative purposes. The only things your baby needs are listed below. Anything else poses a risk of SIDS and suffocation and should be removed anytime the baby is in the crib.

That doesn't mean you can't dress up your crib a little, and there are all sorts of styles and colors of linens to choose from. This is a fun, no-pressure decision—and a chance to express your master decorating skills and exceptional taste!

your basic choices

fitted sheets

A fitted sheet is really your only crib necessity. Most mattresses—and thus most sheets—come in a standard size, but specialty mattresses will require their own sheets. Some manufacturers offer sheets with an elastic band that goes under the mattress to hold them snugly in place.

waterproof mattress pads

Regardless of mattress choice, you'll want to add a waterproof mattress pad under your fitted sheet. It will add a comfortable layer of padding to a mattress already encased in waterproof plastic lining and will help protect premium organic mattresses (which aren't lined) against middle-of-the-night accidents.

antiallergen encasements

All mattresses are prone to dust mites, and crib mattresses are no exception. And since dust mites are the biggest cause of airborne allergies, an antiallergen encasement that goes over the mattress is a good investment. Most adults don't bother with encasements because they're hard to get on and off for washing, but with a baby-size mattress, it's a small effort that's well worth it.

bumpers

Bumpers are more than just decorative: they provide a padded layer that keeps little baby parts from slipping through open rails. While crib styles and safety standards have evolved and bumpers are no longer a necessity, some parents think the crib doesn't look quite fully dressed without one. When your child can pull himself up, you'll want to remove the bumper so he can't use it to climb out.

skirts

Just like a dust ruffle on a full-size bed, crib skirts are purely decorative and completely optional, although they can be great for hiding under-crib storage. The skirt moves with the different mattress settings, though, so when the mattress is at its highest setting, the skirt might not cover up much.

features to look for

snug-fitting. For safety's sake, choose sheets and bumpers that fit snugly.

washable. Make sure everything's machine-washable, even encasements and pads.

health. Babies can spend as much as 70 percent of their first year sleeping, so make your crib a gentle and healthy environment by choosing organic and chemical-free bedding. Sheets are commonly treated with formaldehyde—even baby sheets—but if the package says "Oeko-Tex certified," the sheets are formaldehyde-free.

usage tips

• If you're going to spend the extra money for chemical-free, antiallergen, or organic linens, make sure you also invest in chemical-free, sensitive laundry detergent so you're not adding the chemicals back in.

building your bedding

Once you have all the pieces, how do you put them together? Start with your dust-mite encasement, which you put right on the mattress. Next comes the waterproof mattress pad, then the fitted sheet, which should fit snugly and be completely tucked in.

If you've chosen a bumper, there are special considerations to keep in mind for safety's sake. Tuck your bumper between the mattress and the side of the crib so that only two or three inches are sticking out. (In other words, don't gently set the bumper on top of the mattress like you see in most stores and photographs of beautiful cribs.) This not only improves the airflow at baby's level, it also minimizes the likelihood of little hands and feet getting caught between bumper and mattress. And be sure to attach the bumper securely so that it can't come loose.

Bumpers tie onto crib rails, so attaching them is a little trickier with cribs that have solid ends. You'll need to start and end your ties on a rail side of the crib. Many people who choose this style of crib just skip the bumpers.

What to do with the lovely comforter and pillow sham that came with your crib set? Quilts and comforters can be used as play mats on the floor, hung on the wall, or hung over the crib railing when the baby is not in the crib. And pillows can go on your rocker but should never be left in the crib with your baby. Just because you have them doesn't mean you have to use them! The only thing your baby should have loose in the crib is a lightweight breathable blanket.

• If you use an encasement, be sure to follow the care instructions to ensure that you maintain the allergy-free environment you've started. Most encasements must be washed in hot water and tumble-dried every three weeks.

• Do yourself a favor and have more than one set of the essentials—especially sheets, pads, and blankets. Accidents will happen, and you'll be washing often.

sleeping safety and SIDS

Sudden Infant Death Syndrome (SIDS) is the diagnosis given for the sudden and unexplained death of an infant under one year of age. SIDS is the leading cause of death in children under the age of one, and most cases occur between two and four months of age.

SIDS is sometimes called "crib death" because most cases of SIDS occur when a baby is in a crib, sleeping. Cribs don't cause SIDS, but other aspects of an infant's sleeping environment have been associated with an increased risk. For example, bedding that bunches up around a baby's nose or mouth can cause dangerous re-breathing of oxygen-depleted air.

It's important to make sure that your baby's crib is breathable and that you don't leave unnecessary items in the crib with your child. Other than a fitted sheet and properly installed bumper (see the building your bedding sidebar on page 117), the only thing that should be in the crib with your baby is a lightweight and breathable blanket.

In fact, many SIDS activists prefer a wearable blanket or sleep sack to keep a baby warm at night, replacing loose blankets in the crib and lessening the likelihood of bedding ending up over or around the baby's face.

The American Academy of Pediatrics says that the safest position for babies to sleep in, to reduce the likelihood of SIDS, is on their backs.

If your child likes to roll over in her sleep, consider a sleep positioner that goes next to the hips to keep her properly in place (see the nursery linens section, page 114, for more information on sleep positioners). Some styles also include an inclined back support that keeps the baby's head slightly elevated and can help with digestion or breathing when a baby has a cold. Sleep positioners should not be used once your child can roll over independently.

There is mounting evidence that suggests some babies are more vulnerable to SIDS because of abnormalities found in the part of the brain that controls breathing and waking during sleep. So, while no one knows for sure whether the measures listed above can prevent SIDS, they definitely protect against suffocation and are important precautions to take.

For more information about SIDS organizations, see Resources on page 176.

accessories

sleep positioners. Keep your baby in the recommended position—on his back—with these bumpers that are placed next to the hips: the bumpers keep your baby from rolling onto his front accidentally but should not be used once he starts rolling over on purpose.

wearable blankets. Bedding that bunches up around a baby's face can cause dangerous re-breathing of oxygen-depleted air, a possible cause of SIDS. Wearable blankets replace loose blankets in the crib, lessening the likelihood of infants getting blankets over or around their face.

changing tables

Duty calls—diaper duty, that is. And that duty's going to be calling a lot, up to eighteen times a day during the early months. But look on the bright side: with that much practice, you'll be an expert in no time. The right changing table can make your job easier, providing a safe, convenient, and comfortable space for you to perfect your craft.

Although changing tables are an optional purchase, more parents than not are glad to have a dedicated changing area, especially during the first year. Many parents appreciate the additional height that a changing table offers, which reduces the back strain inherent in parenting. And some parents rely on their changing table so much they buy two, especially if they have a two-story house and want one on each level.

On the other hand, parents who are space-constrained may skip the changing table altogether and use the floor or the end of their bed. It does mean one less thing to buy, but it also means more bending, and supplies that aren't as easily accessible. If you do choose this route, remember: you're also giving up the safety belt, so be extra diligent about keeping one hand on the baby at all times.

your basic choices

Changing tables don't vary much in features or usage. Variations mostly boil down to whether they do or do not have open shelves, drawers, or closed cabinets.

open-shelf style

Your least expensive option in terms of initial investment, the open-shelf changing table is just what it sounds like:

several open shelves. The top one has sturdy guardrails and is made to hold your baby, while the bottom ones hold all the changing accessories.

dresser/changer combo

These units are really dressers with three or four drawers, but they have a changing tray attached to the top that can be removed when the diaper-changing stage has passed. Because you'll use this system longer, it's potentially more economical in the long run.

hybrid

Part changer, part dresser, this hybrid style usually has a changing tray on the top, some dresser drawers, and then some open shelves or a cabinet compartment. This style is also multistage and can serve as bedroom storage for years to come.

general guidance

• The three-shelf changer is the least expensive option and takes up less space, but it's also the least likely to be used once you're past diapers. It's also the easiest for a toddler to climb (although your toddler will figure out a way to climb whatever style you buy). The combos typically cost more and take up more space, but they offer more storage and a longer-term value.

• You'll probably plan your nursery around the crib, which will certainly influence your choice of changing table both in terms of style and how much space you have left. You can often buy a changer that matches the crib; if not, look for one that coordinates nicely.

features to look for

top-shelf space. At the changing table, you should always keep one hand on your baby, so make sure there's room to keep your supplies within easy reach.

storage space. Don't underestimate the need for storage, whether it's for stashing your supplies or to compensate for lack of storage elsewhere in the room.

height. Make sure the changing table is tall enough that you won't have to bend over it, especially if you're prone to back problems. Tables range in height from 32 to 42 inches (approximately 81–107 centimeters), so you should be able to find a comfortable fit at any height.

baby position. Most tables have you changing the baby from the side, but some let you position the baby so he's facing you.

stage considerations

• This is a purchase you'll use a lot during your child's first eighteen months. After that, changing becomes less frequent and starts to take place in varied locations. Expect your child to be potty trained sometime between two and three years old.

lifestyle considerations

multistage. A dresser with a changing tray can be the most expensive, but it will also last the longest, since it can live on in your child's bedroom as storage for years to come.

usage tips

• Always use the safety straps on your changing table or changing pad when changing your baby—that's why they're there!

• Even with the safety straps, never leave your baby unattended on the changing table.

• Make sure your changing pad is surface-cleanable and your changing-pad cover is machine-washable.

• Have at least two changing-pad covers so one can be in the wash at any given time.

• If you want to be sure your changing table is as safe as possible, look for JPMA certification, which recognizes those that have been manufactured with safety in mind.

accessories

changing pads. These pads are what the baby lies on during changes. Vinyl pads are surface-washable and cloth-covered pads are machine-washable; both are waterproof. Some are just a simple, flat pad; others are curved to keep a wiggling baby in place. Most come with a safety belt for extra safety.

changing-pad cover. Protect your changing pad with this extra layer. Covers come in all sorts of styles, colors, and fabrics, from terry to cotton to sherpa. Just make sure yours are machine-washable to get the most out of them.

diaper caddy. Keep your diapering supplies organized and close at hand. There are lots of different styles, but anything with several compartments should do the trick.

diaper pail. The least expensive are plastic, but be careful: they may not be as economical if they require specific refill bags, and you may find they're not airtight enough to keep in odors once your child is on solids. Metal diaper pails cost more, but a really good one can be virtually odor-proof.

rockers and gliders

In the middle of the night, when your baby is inconsolable, few things will be as soothing to both of you as a good rocking session. The gentle motion will help turn tears to sniffles to sleep in no time. And just think how much you'll appreciate not having to pace back and forth with your baby at three in the morning.

But a rocker will be good for more than lulling your child to sleep. It will also be great for middle-of-the-night feedings, and it will eventually become a soothing place for story-time. That said, a rocker is not essential, but for those with the budget and the space, it's definitely nice to have.

your basic choices

rockers
This is a simple concept that needs little introduction—it's any chair that rocks. They come in all kinds of styles, from vintage wooden rocking chairs to the latest in cushioned comfort.

gliders

Most indoor gliders are big, plush, reclining, and specifically designed for parenting. Their gentle gliding motion requires little effort and can be just as soothing as rocking.

general guidance
• This varies by preference, but look for a good rocking or gliding motion. Generally speaking, a gentle and deep motion is more soothing than fast and short. Test for how much noise the chair makes while it's in motion because a squeaking chair is counterproductive when you're trying to rock your baby to sleep.

features to look for
generous seat. Remember, the chair will eventually need to accommodate both you and a growing toddler, who will still want to climb into your lap for soothing and reading.

good headrest. Make sure the headrest is comfortable and high enough to support your head—something you'll value during those sleepy, middle-of-the-night feedings.

adjustable leg-rest. If your chair doesn't have one, a footstool might be a solution, but you'll need to find a leg position that's comfortable for you.

cleanable. Anything that involves a nursing baby means spit-ups and spills, so avoid fabrics that can't be cleaned. Washable slipcovers are also a popular option.

healthy baby, healthy world

From food to textiles, organic and eco-friendly products have become a hot issue—particularly when it comes to children's products. Pound for pound, everything that is harmful to us has an even bigger impact on a tiny person with a developing immune system.

But how do you know what to buy? What's worth the extra expense, and which items are just hopping on the bandwagon? Organic standards are always changing, and you're not alone if the whole thing leaves you feeling confused. But in the meantime, here are some things you can do to create a pure, nontoxic environment for your child that will let everyone breathe a little easier.

• **Sleep better with healthier bedding.** Baby blankets and sheets can contain formaldehyde and other harmful chemicals. Look for organic bedding and Oeko-Tex or IVN-certified fabrics that are both comfortable and healthy.

• **Make sure clean is also healthy.** Babies can be very sensitive to the ammonia, chemicals, and fragrances found in commercial cleaners. There are many nontoxic (and often biodegradable) cleaners to choose from that are both safe and effective.

• **Stock up on simple toys.** Choose simple toys that are PVC-free (meaning no polyvinyl chloride), made of naturally finished wood, or made of washable fabrics.

• **Let in some fresh air.** Make sure your baby's room is well-ventilated, and open the windows to let in fresh air when the weather allows. Be sure to use an air purifier to help minimize dust and other irritants.

stage considerations

• A rocker is great for the nursing and bottle-feeding stage, but its usefulness doesn't end there. It can help with nighttime soothing at any age and live on as a favorite chair for story-time.

lifestyle considerations

space. Gliders in particular can be big, so more streamlined rockers present a better option for the space-constrained. Either way, make sure you measure before you buy.

accessories

ottoman or footstool. Although you should be able to sit comfortably with your feet on the ground, these will help you find an even more comfortable position to alleviate back strain.

equipment bag. Sort of like a "stuff" holder that hangs off your glider, this helps keep you from having to get up mid-snuggle. Use these to stash extra burp cloths and binkies, and maybe even a bottle of water or magazine for you.

baby monitors

Short of standing over your child's crib while she sleeps, nothing can give you more peace of mind than a good baby monitor. The moment your baby cries, whimpers, or even stirs, you'll be able to hear her and come to her aid. And it's not only about peace of mind—it's about nabbing a little bit of time for yourself. A monitor allows you to go about your day while still keeping one eye (or at least an ear) on your child. There will be plenty of time for minding your own business when your child is older, but during the early days, enjoy this opportunity to eavesdrop with impunity!

your basic choices

While features and options vary widely by model, there are two basic types of baby monitors.

audio monitors

These allow you to listen for stirring or crying, so you'll know the moment your baby wakes up. Most include a visual sound display, which will alert you even if you've turned the volume down too low to hear.

video monitors

With a video monitor, you never have to wonder whether your child is sleeping. A small video display lets you keep an eye on your child just as if you were standing right there. These monitors also offer night vision, so you're never in the dark.

general guidance

• Monitors have a base transmitter for the baby's room and a receiving unit for the parent. Depending on the model, the receiver either stays in one location, such as your bedroom, or is portable, so you can take it wherever you need. Obviously, the portable receivers give you greater flexibility.

• Monitors are prone to interference, especially in densely populated areas. Try a more powerful monitor—a 900MHz/2.4GHz model is good—and look for a unit with multiple channels. The only way you can really tell if you'll get a good, interference-free operating range is to try it out at home, so be sure to save your receipt until you've tested it.

features to look for

intercom. The sound of your voice can be reassuring for a crying infant, and, as your child grows into a toddler, the intercom will allow you to communicate from different rooms.

rechargeable battery or AC adapter. Don't run out of power! Look for monitors with rechargeable batteries and/or AC adapters.

out-of-battery signal. This indicates if your monitor is running out of juice so you can plug it in.

out-of-range signal. If you've wandered too far from your handset to pick up the signal, an audio alert will let you know right away.

thermostat. You should always pay attention to the temperature in your baby's nursery, and a monitor that includes a temperature reading can save an extra purchase.

Sure, playtime is fun. And we know it's important for a child's physical and cognitive development. It's also an important activity for you—not just for your general sense of merriment, but also because it gives you a little break. Here are some favorite activities for both babies and toddlers that will keep them entertained so you can breathe for a moment.

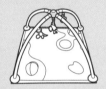

• **Activity mats.** From day one, you'll welcome tummy-time with your little one, and an activity mat with a little padding provides the proper foundation. Some mats take the concept a step further by adding texture, colors, and accessories for developing important skills. The more deluxe options even offer accessories, to be rotated in at different ages, which ensure continued development (and keep your baby interested). Pick one that's easy to put away in case you need a break from baby decor.

• **Bouncers and rockers.** A bouncing seat or small rocking lounger that cradles your child and provides soothing motion can be a lifesaver. Some are simple and can be operated with an occasional nudge from your foot. Others are battery-powered extravaganzas that come equipped with lights, sounds, and music. (Just make sure the extra features are soothing rather than irritating.) If you're not sure which route to take, decide whether you want a seat that amuses your child or one that makes him sleepy. Whatever your choice, make sure it's easily washable.

• **Swings.** Although less common than rockers or bouncers, swings are another potential source of amusement—not the kind of swing you put in your yard, mind you, but a smaller, freestanding swing set meant to go indoors. Swings can be cumbersome, and not everyone can afford the space. Further, while some babies adore swings and love falling asleep in them, others seem to feel ambivalent, so try before you buy, if possible.

• **Activity centers.** Once your child is walking—or at least teetering—she'll want to use her newfound skill as much as possible. And while learning to walk is an exciting time for baby, it's a busy one for you, so get a little help from an activity center. These are part walker and part moving play table, and they provide the support your child needs to move about unassisted. Like swings, they take up a lot of room, but you can easily find a model that collapses for between-use storage.

• **Jumpers.** There's nothing like watching a baby, giddy with glee, bouncing up and down in a simple jumper that suspends from a doorway. Some babies are halfhearted bouncers, though, so test-drive a friend's jumper, if possible. If you do decide to buy one, make sure it will fit into your intended space.

• **Books, music, and other toys.** From board books to chapter books, classical music to baby rock, teething rings to stackers, there are all sorts of activities that are both fun and developmentally stimulating. With no shortage of tips (and gifts) from friends and family, you'll have plenty to choose from. Pay attention to age recommendations, but know that no two kids are exactly alike: only you can know for sure what's right for your child.

motion sensor. Placed under the crib mattress, these sensors signal an alarm if the baby doesn't stir for a longer-than-normal period.

usage tips

• Monitors don't replace supervision; common sense regarding parental care still applies.

• Don't be surprised if you pick up other voices (often neighbors, so be careful). Remember, changing channels can help. For more privacy, consider a digital monitor with encoded signals.

• This is an electrical gadget; keep it clear of water and follow the manufacturer's guidelines.

• Want to really keep an eye on things? A video monitor can also double as a nanny-cam.

products for feeding

some people put a lot of care and energy into what they eat; others just grab whatever's handy. But, suddenly, there's a baby to think about, and none of the same rules apply. There are a million decisions to be made, both big and small, starting from day one.

First you'll need to decide whether to breast-feed, bottle-feed, or both. Most parents end up supplementing one choice with the other, even if only temporarily, and you'll probably fall somewhere on a spectrum, too.

Before you know it, you'll be introducing solids. While that means new freedom for the breast-feeding mom, it also means a lot more new stuff. This stage is busy, entertaining, difficult, and above all else, messy. Preparation, organization, lots of cleanup, and a good sense of humor are all important ingredients.

Not to worry, though, feeding becomes second nature pretty quickly. In the meantime, let's take a look at what you'll need to keep your kitchen stocked and your baby's tummy full.

............bottles and nipples.................

Unless you're available for breast-feeding 24/7, you're going to need bottles. Whether they're full of breast milk or formula is up to you—and what kind you end up using is pretty much up to your baby.

There are a myriad of combinations of bottles and nipples, including different shapes and materials for both. Will your baby like a bent-neck plastic bottle with a realistic silicone nipple? Or will he prefer a straight-neck disposable bottle with a traditional latex nipple?

All babies are different, and they'll actually have clear preferences, easily taking to some bottles and not to others. It will soon become clear that your baby is the ultimate decision maker, so don't over-invest in any one approach until you've figured out what works.

your basic choices

There are plenty of options, and we'll cover those in a minute. But the first decision to be made is what style of bottle you want.

reusable plastic bottles

Reusable plastic bottles get filled, used, cleaned, and used again. The most popular choice among parents, these bottles don't break, are typically less expensive, and are easy to find.

disposable bottles

This option consists of a non-disposable holder and disposable bags. Though less ecologically sound, this is a more convenient choice for quick cleanup. And, if you have a breast pump that uses a disposable-bottle system, you can transfer your milk from pump to bottle without losing a drop.

reusable glass bottles

There's a growing population that believes glass is healthier for delivering milk. Of course, the drawback with glass—even tempered for use by babies—is that it's both easier to break and heavier. Where you stand in this debate is 100 percent personal. Ask your pediatrician if you want an expert opinion.

general guidance

• Start with the choices that fit your personal lifestyle and philosophy, but be flexible and try out different bottle/nipple combinations. There's no point in pushing what doesn't work. In the end, your favorite will be the one your child takes to the most.

• Another important thing to keep in mind: nothing will drive you crazier than a bottle that leaks, so make sure the brand you choose seals well before you stock up.

features to look for

neck styles. Reusable bottles have two different neck styles to choose from: straight or bent. Some parents feel straight necks are easier for switching between breast- and bottle-feeding; others argue that bent-neck bottles minimize air intake during nursing. Consult with your pediatrician, and listen to your baby, too.

nipple materials. Silicone nipples (the clear ones) are firmer and hold their shape longer, while latex (the amber-colored ones) are softer but may not hold up as well over time. Babies often prefer one over the other, making your choice simple.

nipple shapes. There are three nipple shapes to consider: traditional, orthodontic, or realistic. Traditional nipples have the regular protruding shape that you normally see. Orthodontic nipples are flat on the side that rests against the tongue. Realistic nipples—some of which are also considered orthodontic—are flatter and designed to mimic a mother's nipple, making it easier to switch between breast- and bottle-feeding.

nipple size. One size does not fit all. Start small for newborns and go bigger for toddlers. Experiment till you find the right fit.

nipple flow rates. Nipples come with different flow rates, based on your baby's age. Check the packaging to be sure you've got the right one.

stage considerations

The ideal nipple for your baby is typically defined by her age (although some doctors advise breast-feeding moms to stick with a first-stage nipple). Part of the equation is the size of the nipple, but flow rate is also an important factor. You can either buy different nipples for different stages, or find nipples that adjust accordingly.

usage tips

• Milk should drip, not pour. If the milk comes out in a steady stream, it's time to replace the nipple.

• Never microwave milk or formula. After heating the milk, do the old inner wrist trick to make sure it's the right temperature—typically room temperature, never hot.

• Newborns need their bottles sterilized, but at some point you can just start washing bottles in the dishwasher. Some people only sterilize for a month, while others sterilize for two years. Consult your pediatrician for an expert opinion on when you can make the switch.

accessories

bottle-cleaning brush. This is an essential item for keeping your bottles clean and ready for use.

insulated bottle carriers. Keep your bottles at the optimal temperature anytime you're out and about with a portable bottle carrier. These can carry anywhere from a single to a four-pack of bottles.

bottle-storage rack. A good bottle storage rack or bottle tree will help you dry and store bottles easily between feedings.

bottle warmers. A nifty kitchen accessory that helps ensure you're serving your milk at the perfect temperature for your baby.

bottle sterilizers. Since newborn baby bottles should always be sterilized, a bottle sterilizer is a handy tool, and an easy alternative to boiling water on the stove.

·············breast pumps·······················

If you've ever seen a woman shopping for a breast pump, you're probably familiar with that dazed look that's a cross between *How do I know which one to buy?* and *You want me to do what with that thing?* But choosing a breast pump is really pretty simple once you know what you need; as for that second issue, well, that's just something that takes a little getting used to.

You may not even need a breast pump—especially if you're planning on going the formula route. If you'll be breast-feeding, it all depends on how much you'll be away from home. Working moms? Definitely. Stay-at-home moms? Not so much.

Pumps can be expensive—topping out at a few hundred dollars for advanced models—but there are choices for every budget. You do, however, get what you pay for, so consider how you'll be using it before deciding.

You may want to consider renting a machine to try before you buy, or if you have a short-term need for more capacity or more efficient pumping. Renting might also be a good solution if you start pumping later, since you won't be using it as long.

your basic choices

Breast pumps all work in basically the same way: they use suction to draw milk from the breast into a container. What varies is how powerful the suction is and whether it's provided manually or with a motor. There are three basic types of breast pumps to consider.

full-size motorized pump

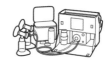

These are the most powerful pumps, and they get the job done quickly and efficiently. They're more expensive than other pumps but probably worth the investment if pumping will be part of your daily routine.

portable motorized pump

These pumps are smaller and lighter than a full-size pump and made to go where you go. Some are battery operated, some are electric, and some offer the convenience of both.

hand-pump

These manually controlled pumps are lightweight, small, and inexpensive—and really all you'll need if you just want an occasional backup bottle or to express milk to relieve pressure.

general guidance

• When it comes to choosing your breast pump, the first question to ask yourself is how often you'll need it. Are you just looking for an occasional night out, or are you a working mom who has to store milk every day? The more you'll rely on your pump to keep up the milk supply, the more you'll want to spend. Ditto if you're planning on having more than one child and will be using it over the course of several years.

• Don't be tempted to skimp. The better the pump, the easier pumping will be and the better you'll feel about it. And while some women are able to get a good flow going with any pump, most find that higher-quality pumps help them produce milk more easily. However, if you're just looking for a way to store up a little milk for an occasional outing (maybe even a date night!), then an inexpensive hand pump should be just fine, as long as it fits comfortably and works reasonably well.

features to look for

ac adaptor. Battery-operated pumps are convenient, but an AC adaptor is a good extra in case you run out of power.

adjustable suction and speed control. This feature allows you to ease into pumping in the early days, then maximize efficiency as your breasts get used to it.

easy to clean. You could be pumping six or more times a day if you're working away from home, so look for easy-to-clean options when considering your pick.

size/weight. Make sure your pump is portable enough, small enough, and light enough to work for you.

double-pumping. Breast-pumping takes about the same amount of time as breast-feeding, but a model that pumps both breasts at once should cut your time in half.

lifestyle considerations

portability. Will you be carrying your pump around with you, or will you store it in the same place you use it? Make sure the model you choose is portable enough for your lifestyle. And if you're a mom on the go, make sure there are adequate power options (either batteries or a car's cigarette-lighter plug) so that you don't have to be chained to a wall plug.

style. Does the case scream "breast pump," and, if so, do you care? There are plenty of camouflage styles that look like everyday briefcases, purses, and backpacks to help you be discreet.

usage tips

• Pumping will probably feel weird at first, but it does get better. Start on lower speeds with less suction and build up to higher speeds after you get used to it.

• Pumping might be uncomfortable, but it shouldn't actually hurt. If you find pumping painful, try adjusting the suction; if that doesn't work, consult your doctor.

• Like breast-feeding, most people now realize that pumping is a fact of life. Where and when you pump is a matter of personal preference (and modesty), but you certainly don't have to hide in a bathroom stall to do it.

• If you're a working mom, you'll need to gauge the appropriateness of pumping at your desk, as well as your comfort level in doing so. Fortunately, most larger companies now have pumping stations to allow nursing mothers their privacy.

• A nursing poncho lets you go about your business without having to hold a blanket over yourself with one hand.

accessories

breast products. There are breast creams that heal chafing, bra pads to prevent leaking, and plastic shells that form

breast-feeding vs. formula

Making the choice to breast-feed or bottle-feed is a big decision. If this is your first child, it's important to go into the whole thing with an open mind. Some moms feel strongly about nursing but then aren't able to. Some are sure they'll bottle-feed but end up nursing. Most parents will find that it's not exactly black and white and that there's a place in their life for both methods.

Your body is made for nursing, even if it doesn't quite feel like it at first. Even though nursing is a natural process, it takes practice, patience, and getting used to—from adjusting to your baby's needs to building up calluses where you never thought calluses should be. It's also one of the most intimate times a mother will share with her baby, and a lot of parents today feel strongly about the benefits of natural breast milk.

For some moms, however, breast-feeding just isn't a match. Maybe you simply can't produce enough milk. Maybe your schedule doesn't allow for it. Or maybe it's just not a good fit. In these cases, thank goodness for modern science and formula.

Most moms are lucky enough to get to choose where they fall on the spectrum, and there are products to support them no matter what their preference. Just go light on purchases until you get through the first few weeks. Only then will you know the combination of products that will suit you best.

a protective layer when your breasts are too tender even for your bra.

milk storage. Whether it's extra bottles, freezer trays, or disposable bags, you'll want extras for stocking up.

breast-pump wipes. Quick and convenient, this is a great solution for cleaning your breast pump, and you can take them along anywhere.

microwave bags. For quick and simple cleanup of your breast pump and feeding accessories, microwave bags are quicker than boiling and more effective than dishwashing. Just add water and heat in the microwave.

freezer storage. When you need to stock up on extra breast milk, try freezable containers that are compatible with your pump, or a breast-milk storage tray that looks like an ice tray with a lid.

bottle-storage bags. If you're away from home or need to keep your breast milk cool in transit, get an insulated bag for easy storage.

.....feeding support pillows.................

When you're feeding your baby, finding a comfortable position can be a challenge. Your lap isn't high enough for proper support, and holding your baby in your arms can start to feel like some sort of weird endurance test.

A rounded feeding or nursing pillow that fits around your waist can help support your child at the proper elevation, making your job a lot easier and saving you from cramped arms. Position is especially important for breast-feeding moms, and these pillows let you easily navigate the perfect elevation for achieving a good "latch"—the key to productive and comfortable breast-feeding.

your basic choices

There are two different styles of feeding pillows, plus a minimalist option that utilizes an everyday pillow.

horseshoe style

Just as the name implies, these pillows are shaped like a horseshoe and fit partway around your waist, allowing you to sit on a couch or rocker while you nurse.

doughnut style

The doughnut style reaches farther around your waist than the horseshoe and has a strap that latches in back. The strap holds the pillow in place so you can walk around with it, but still allows you to lean back when seated. The trade-off for some is the boxier shape and firmer feel that's a little less pillowlike.

regular pillow

If you really don't want to add yet another thing to the pile of baby stuff, you could get away with using a regular pillow. It won't offer the customized fit and support of the other two options, but it can be used for other purposes.

features to look for

machine-washable. Breast-feeding pillows get dirty. Look for a removable, washable cover, and consider picking up a spare one for busy wash-days.

multiple-capacity. If you have twins or multiples, look for special versions created just for you.

storage pockets. To keep essentials close at hand, some pillows offer cargo space in the form of pockets for stashing goods.

stage considerations

A horseshoe-style feeding pillow can enjoy a second life when your child is learning to sit up. Just as you would wrap the pillow around your front to support the baby, you can wrap the pillow around your baby's backside to give her a little extra support during the wobbly early stage of sitting.

high chairs

As soon as you start introducing solids, your baby will need a place to sit during meals. He won't be ready for a dining-room chair right away—and you won't be ready for the dining-room mess!

This is another product that we recommend buying new. As lovely as your grandmother's old high chair might be, antique and vintage chairs weren't made with today's safety standards in mind. In fact, they can actually be dangerous.

For example, most older models don't come with a five-point harness. Many of them have wider seats, as well, making it easier for a child to slip through. If you're going to go the secondhand route, just make sure it's a fairly recent model chair that will keep your child safe and secure.

your basic choices

Whether it's a standard high chair, a European-style chair, a portable seat, or a booster, there is a wide range of styles available.

standard high chair

This is your standard, everyday chair with a tray. These can be used as soon as the child is sitting (at about six months), and some reclining models can be used even earlier.

european-style high chair

These chairs don't have trays, allowing you to bring the baby right up to the table with you, starting at about nine months. As a general rule, this style can be used beyond the high chair stage as a toddler seat.

hybrid

These chairs have trays and can be used as early as six months, but they also grow into a toddler chair. They tend to look more like furniture and go well in dining rooms. The trade-off is that they don't have all the features of standard high chairs.

portable high chair

Whether you are traveling, need a backup seat for Grand-ma's house, or just don't have enough room for a standard high chair, this compact seat that clips onto your table or chairs is an easy solution.

booster seat

Sometime after about 18 months, your child will make the transition to a booster seat. This is the modern version of using a telephone book to help your child reach the table, but it comes equipped with a seat-belt to keep squirming youngsters in place.

chair harness

Not technically a chair, this fabric seat-cover ties to the back of a chair and has safety straps to anchor your child in place. This style is extremely easy to travel with, but doesn't pro-vide the boost that a true booster seat does.

general guidance

If you buy a standard high chair, keep in mind that its useful life won't be all that long, although you'll enjoy its special features during the early stages. At some point, your tod-dler will need to move to a booster seat or a European-style toddler chair, and this can happen as early as 18 months for some children.

No matter what type of chair you buy, here are some factors to consider.

size. How much room do you have, and how much room does your chair of choice require? Make sure these two measurements add up.

stability. As a general rule, the wider the base of the high chair, the more stable it will be. Make sure yours will stay standing through hectic mealtimes.

washability. There's no way around it: high chairs get dirty. No matter what kind you choose, make sure it's easy to clean, and definitely avoid fabrics that will stain or require a lot of maintenance.

If you're buying a portable high chair, you have two different styles to choose from: one that clips onto your table, or one that clips onto your chairs.

portable that secures to table. These have become so popular, some families buy them instead of a regular high chair. You just have to make sure it fits onto your table and won't damage it. Although these are as secure as standard high chairs, be sure to adhere to weight limits to ensure the chair's stability as your child grows. Best for travel are the fabric seats on a collapsible frame that fold and pack flat.

portable that secures to chairs. These use the legs of a chair for elevation, and can be as complex as a mini–high chair, with all the same features, including a tray. Because these seats don't pack flat, fewer people choose them as a portable option. However, because this style is smaller than a full-size, it can be great as a second chair to be kept at Grandma's for part-time use.

features to look for

five-point harness. This is a must for keeping your baby securely in place during the high chair stage. In the booster seat stage, the harness is optional, but recommended.

seat-adjustability. Babies come in all different shapes and sizes, and those shapes and sizes will change rapidly, so pick a high chair that will grow with and adjust to your baby at every stage.

adjustable footrest. The footrest should be movable to accommodate your growing baby.

height-adjustability. This setting lets you move the seat to whatever height allows you to comfortably reach your baby, whether you're sitting or standing.

one-hand maneuverability. From latches to seat-belts to adjustments, the more you can do while holding a plate of macaroni and cheese in one hand, the better. This is especially true of the tray.

collapsibility. If you don't have a lot of room to leave a high chair sitting out, find one that folds up for easy between-meal storage.

recline settings. If the chair reclines, you can start your child in it earlier, rather than waiting till she can sit up. It will also come in handy for the child who enjoys a quick snooze immediately after eating.

locking mechanism. If you pick a high chair with wheels, make sure that you can lock the wheels into place, for obvious reasons.

extra functions. Some high chairs can do double duty as rocking chairs, bouncy seats, or swings, saving you a purchase and meaning one less thing for you to store.

stage considerations

• A standard high chair provides adequate support for the sitting baby as early as six months. You can start using a European-style chair when the baby is able to sit totally unassisted and without support, usually around nine months.

• European-style chairs are meant to grow with your child, and many are designed so they can be used indefinitely.

• By about age two, most children have progressed past standard high chairs and have moved into the land of toddler or booster seats, depending on the child and the parent. The focus then moves away from safety and becomes more about getting your baby through the meal without distractions.

• How long your child will need a booster seat depends mostly on his size and your tolerance for messes. If he can reach the table and sit still throughout the meal, he's earned his way out of the booster.

lifestyle considerations

space. Space-constrained parents might want to consider a collapsible high chair that folds up for storage between meals. If you're really cramped, consider the minimalist approach: a portable clip-on seat that can easily be folded.

multistage. Hybrids and European styles are multistage, and if you don't mind the minimalist approach, portables are, too.

portability. The most travel-friendly seating option is the collapsible, cloth seat that clips onto the table. If your child is tall enough to reach the table, consider the harness belting system for secure seating.

style. High chair choices are driven as much by aesthetics as anything else, so choose what will fit best into your home. Some look more like actual, adult furniture, while others have more of a molded-plastic, baby-gear feel.

usage tips

• If you prefer using a dishwasher to hand-washing, pick a high chair with a spare feeding tray.

• Use the five-point harness for safety—and resist the temptation to stop buckling up your child when she starts getting bigger and looking more stable.

• A slightly reclined seat can be great for bottle-feeding and is a necessity until the baby can sit upright without any help.

• Keep sharp, hot, and dangerous items out of reach of the high chair, especially in the kitchen. Even while seated, kids can be amazingly fast and agile!

• High chairs are for sitting, not standing. Of course, if your child's five-point harness is always secured, this should be easy to enforce.

• Double-check that the chair is locked into place when you use it, especially if the chair is collapsible.

• Never leave your baby unattended in any type of high chair or booster.

• Do a bib check. If you're using anything other than cloth (such as rubber), double-check that the bib fits with the high chair tray and doesn't create discomfort for the child.

accessories

seat cushions and covers. While most high chairs come with some type of detachable seat cushion, some don't. Even those that do could use a backup.

splash mats. Made to go under the high chair and catch whatever falls, a splash mat can save your floors. They also make cleanup a whole lot easier, saving you a lot of vacuuming, mopping, or carpet shampooing.

High chair–friendly dishes. Make sure the dishes you choose fit within the tray, and look for ones with "sticky" bottoms to help keep them in place.

dishes

Bye-bye breast-feeding, hello solids! When babies start eating real food, they use a lot of the same dishes we do, just in smaller sizes. From plates and bowls to utensils and cups, they get their very own special place setting. Technically, your baby can share some of the dishes you use, but dinnertime will be a bigger success if he has tools designed especially for small, not-yet-dexterous hands.

your basic choices

When it's time to set the table for the smaller members of the family, you'll probably need one or more of each of the following.

plates and bowls

Your child's dishware—both plates and bowls—should be

designed to make scooping easy. Look for plates that look more like a bowl, with higher edges for easy scooping and a sturdier base than most bowls provide. Ideally, they'll also come with fitted, microwave-safe lids for easy warm-ups.

cups

Start your child off with a training cup that has a lid and two handles for easy gripping. Next comes the sippy cup—those ubiquitous lidded cups with spouts to mitigate spills. Eventually, your child will graduate to an open-top cup with no lid. Just make sure the cup is small enough to hold and has a sturdy base to discourage spills.

baby spoons

Oh, if only it were as simple as one lovely silver spoon. In the "here comes the airplane" phase, you'll want a long-handled spoon with a small, soft rubber scoop that's ideal for baby's toothless mouth. When your baby starts wanting to feed herself, look for short, soft spoons that make scooping easy.

toddler utensils

At some point, after your baby has mastered the use of his own spoon, he'll start asking for utensils like yours. Now is the time to introduce toddler utensils: small-size forks, spoons, and (eventually) knives. Look for forgiving prongs and generous spoon ladles with metal ends and soft handles. You can even find starter chopsticks that can enhance dexterity.

to-go containers

These single-serving snack containers have a lid with a small opening that only lets a few snacks escape at a time—no more dumping the crackers all over the backseat!

general guidance

• When it comes to pint-size dishes and utensils, there's no one perfect choice—though there are lots of good options. The key is practicality. Think about what will work best for someone with smaller hands, a lack of coordination, and a tendency to spill things.

• Try a few brands before you stock up, and keep in mind that what you'll need when you first introduce solids will be different from what you'll need just a few months later. Choose smaller-size everything, and make sure plates and bowls will fit on your child's high chair tray without teetering on the rim.

features to look for

nonbreakable. Who would make a breakable child's dish? Believe it or not, they exist, so make sure you choose something that can hold up to abuse.

leak-resistant. This one is for the sippy cups. Try one before you buy many, and make sure they do their job keeping spills to a minimum. (Some even have a no-spill feature that prevents them from leaking from the spout when they're on their side.)

easy to clean. Make sure the dishes are easy for you to clean, whether that means dishwasher-safe or just simple to hand-wash.

slip-proof. With plates, bowls, and cups, look for a sticky backing that keeps them from sliding around. If your baby likes to throw dishes, look for stronger suction backing.

Baby food in a jar is certainly convenient, but more and more parents are hungry for easy, fresh options that they can make themselves. If you want to do some of the cooking yourself, here are a few products that will turn you into a baby-food gourmand.

food mill

Sure, you can use a fork to mash up baby food in a bowl, but it's tricky to get a smooth consistency. A food mill is a minor investment that will make your job a whole lot easier. The portable kind comes apart easily for cleaning and is dishwasher safe. You can also buy an electric model that's more like a food processor: super fast and efficient, but more expensive and trickier to clean. Either way, this handy little gadget will be a kitchen fixture for years to come.

cookbooks

Start with an instructional feeding book that gives you techniques for introducing solids. More than a cookbook, it can offer instructions for pureeing and mashing, advice for introducing tastes, strategies for sequencing and mixing foods, and ideas for preparation, storage, and serving

Early-stage cookbooks can help you make meals that are meant especially for kids, with kid-size portions and tastes. Then come family-focused cookbooks, for when you want to stop making separate mini meals and start making meals that work for the whole family. There are also specialty cookbooks that take on a narrower approach, focusing on things like organic foods or cooking with a food allergy in mind.

storage

Freezer storage is essential for the adventurous parent who wants to serve fresh food but doesn't always have the time to prepare it. One great solution is a stackable, space-efficient storage container that looks like an ice tray with a lid. An organized parent can go to the farmers' market on the weekend, puree a variety of fruits and veggies, and stock the freezer with microwave-ready single servings.

bibs

Picture your child's favorite outfit. Now picture it covered in jelly, drool, finger paint, or grape juice. Not so cute anymore, is it? A bib can save the day by providing an extra layer of protection, and consistent use can save you a lot of laundry angst.

Thrifty parents can purchase a clipping device that allows them to make a bib out of a washcloth, napkin, cloth diaper, or dish towel. These are especially handy for people on the go who want to travel with less.

Bibs are inexpensive, so it's tempting to buy a bunch of them, but make sure you like what you're buying and that they fit (they should be snug but not tight). Test out one or two styles you think you'll like before you invest.

your basic choices

There is a wide range of bibs to choose from.

drool bibs

Until they've started eating solids, babies don't need a full bib, but these smaller bibs protect the chest from drool and the occasional bottle drip. Drool bibs are almost always made of cloth since they're worn for longer periods of time, though some have waterproof backing.

standard bibs

These are your standard, everyday bibs that cover baby from neck to tummy during mealtime—a necessity during this deliriously messy stage.

smock-style bibs

These provide generous coverage and protect fronts, sides, even sleeves. Some styles pull over the head, while others tie at the back. All can do double duty as art smocks.

molded-plastic bibs

These sturdy bibs provide excellent protection because they stay in place, have fitted necklines, and repel rather than absorb liquids. A big bonus of this style is that they can be rinsed right off for easy cleanup.

disposable bibs

Great for road trips or eating out, these present an on-the-go option that simplifies packing and cleanup.

features to look for

washability. Good bibs will last a long time and get washed again and again. Cloth should be machine-washable—no dry cleaning!—and other materials should be easy to wipe clean.

materials. Cloth bibs are comfortable and machine-washable. Surface-wipe bibs are made from machine-washable fabric but have a special coating that makes them easier to wipe clean. Plastic bibs rinse off and are more durable, but sacrifice cuteness and possibly comfort.

catchall pockets. Some bibs offer a pocket at the bottom to catch food that would otherwise end up on the floor. Look for wide pockets that stay open on their own (the better to gobble up dropped crumbs with).

easy to secure. Bibs secure behind the child's neck with snaps, ties, or hook-and-loop fasteners. Any of these are fine choices; just make sure they stay secured when they need to and remove easily when you're done.

products for bath-time

everyone loves that new-baby smell, but it does require some maintenance. In the early days, bathing is simple. Less is more, and that includes both the frequency of baths and the number of products you use. Warm water and a washcloth go a long way, since your child won't be doing much more than sleeping, eating, and thinking deep baby thoughts.

As your baby starts to grow, bath-time will become more important. Happily, it's a great time for bonding, and it just gets more fun as your child grows older.

bathtubs

Babies don't need a lot of washing—really only every few days. You won't give your baby a true bath until after the umbilical cord falls off. The best place to bathe your newborn is in the kitchen sink because it's easier on your back and lets you feel more in control. Needless to say, at some point your child will start to outgrow the sink, and then it's time to transition to the tub.

The first few baths can be scary, but a bath seat or an infant tub that fits inside the sink or bathtub will help ensure your slippery little baby is secure. Though you'll only use your infant tub or seat for a few months, it's well worth the money in terms of peace of mind.

your basic choices

The first three choices are the most common, and all are made to work inside your sink or tub.

sink tub

For newborns and infants, you can use a reclining tub that fits inside your kitchen sink and allows you to stand while bathing your child. Though not absolutely essential, this tub is relatively inexpensive and saves you a lot of fumbling and worry.

bathtub insert

Designed to sit inside of a regular tub, these smaller tubs are quicker to fill than the whole tub and also more secure, since there's less room for your child to slip around in. There are reclining options for younger children and adjustable options that take you from reclining to seated for longer-term use.

bath seats

A bath seat isn't a tub, but rather a seat that sits inside a filled sink or tub to hold your child upright in the water. There are styles for infants, styles for older babies, and styles that cover both. In general, bath seats are more compact than tub inserts, and many even collapse for easy storage when not in use.

Though not as popular (or easy to find), there are two other baby bath solutions, used in other countries and starting to gain popularity in the United States.

buckets

While bathing your baby in a bucket might sound less than dignified, the new generation of bath buckets hold your baby in the proper position for bathing and have received critical acclaim in other countries for their safety benefits and compact style.

slings

Just as it sounds, this tool cradles your baby in a reclining position in the sink or tub and is best suited for newborns and infants.

general guidance

• First and foremost, you'll want a tub you feel safe using. Make sure the tub or seat is stable, and look for nonslip surfaces, both inside and on the bottom of the tub. (A caveat: no matter how safe your tub is, never leave your child unattended while bathing.)

• Make sure the tub or seat holds your baby in the proper position: with head above water but body covered so she doesn't get cold.

• Look for a low-maintenance tub that's easy to wipe down so you can keep it clean from mildew. The more cracks and crevices the tub has, the longer the cleanup process and the easier it is to miss a spot.

• While there's something to be said for investing in one tub that grows with your baby, it's going to take up more room. If you're space-constrained or will be sharing a bathroom with your child, you might prefer to make a couple of purchases that cover different stages but are more compact.

features to look for

drainage. Lifting a tubful of water to dump it out can be difficult—especially with a toddler tub. Save yourself the effort by getting one with a drain.

water-temperature gauge. Keep an eye on water temperature with a thermometer that's either built in or added as an accessory (although you should always check the temperature yourself to make sure it's not too hot).

water-line delineator. A simple water-fill line inside the tub helps make sure you keep your baby covered without overfilling.

mildew-resistant. Keep your tub from becoming a health hazard with a mildew-resistant fabrication.

stage considerations

Sink seats are among the most popular choices for infants but aren't made to hold toddlers. By about six months, most kids will graduate to the tub, when the full range of options comes into play. It's hard to say when your child will graduate out of baby tubs altogether—every child is different, and so is every tub—but it generally happens sometime after age two.

lifestyle considerations

space. Seats are often more collapsible than tubs, so if you're sharing a bathroom with your baby, you might want something you can put away. (Just keep in mind that they do use a lot more water, since you're still filling the whole tub!)

portability. If you travel a lot, you might want both a tub for home and something more portable, such as a collapsible seat.

multistage. Tubs are more likely to be multistage than seats, and some models can take you all the way from infant to toddler. Seats can also be multistage but will only cover stages after your baby is sitting.

usage tips

• When bathing, start with your baby's body, work your way to the face, then end with the hair (because a wet head can be chilly!).

• Nothing takes the fun out of bath-time like the shivers, so keep the area where you're bathing and changing your baby warm and cozy.

accessories

faucet covers. Kids seem destined to have head-on collisions with the faucet, but a rubber faucet cover can make the difference between a minor boo-boo and an occasion for stitches.

floating thermometers. Make sure the baby's bath is juuuuust right. These come in all sorts of fun styles, too, like floating flowers or ducks.

handheld sprayer. If bubble bath becomes a bath-time favorite, a sprayer that hooks onto your faucet can simplify rinsing at the end.

rinsing cups. These are handy for tears-free hair rinsing—especially if you don't have a handheld sprayer.

washcloths and sponges. Look for small and simple natural sponges or soft organic cloths. We recommend soft, natural sponges because they make it easy to wash tiny body parts.

hooded towels. A must for babies, these cover both the head and body for easy and quick dry-offs.

bath toys. From rubber duckies to bath squirters, bath toys are a staple of bath-time. At the beginning, your baby will have more fun with you, but as she becomes more aware of her surroundings, she'll really start enjoying her toys, too.

toy-holders. Whether it's a handy scoop for easy cleanup or a mesh bag that hangs in the shower, these will keep your bathroom tidy and keep you from stepping on plastic sea creatures every time you get in the shower. Just make sure the holder drains so toys have a chance to dry.

stool. This one's for you so you don't constantly have to kneel over the tub.

......skin- and hair-care........................

Once the early days of warm water and a washcloth have passed, you'll want to seek out products that have been specially formulated for children, since adult formulas contain ingredients that can be hard on your little one's sensitive skin. When you can, choose natural or organic products, and keep things as simple as possible.

Beyond basic care, some babies have skin issues that need special attention. Most of the more common skin ailments, like cradle cap and eczema, can be addressed with simple, nonprescription products.

Remember, even though bathing your baby is a necessity, it's also a great opportunity for you to have fun together. So get ready to embrace bubbles, squirters, and cute little hooded towels—this might just turn out to be one of your favorite parts of parenting!

your basic choices

These products will keep your child looking fresh and smelling sweet, while keeping skin soft and healthy.

foam wash

This is a gentle formula, just for newborns, that is usually soap-free and used to gently cleanse both hair and body.

two-in-one wash

Like foam wash, this product does double duty as both shampoo and body wash, but it comes in formulas for both newborns and older babies.

soap and body wash

Whether you use bar soap or body wash is your choice, but you'll want something a little more effective as your child becomes more active.

shampoos and conditioners

These are just like the products you use, only gentler. For those who live in cold climates, leave-in conditioners can help dry hair and scalps.

hair products

As baby's hair grows longer and fuller, a good de-tangler can save you from snarls; a light hair gel for kids will make baby-fine hair do your bidding.

bubble bath and bath milk

Every kid loves bubble bath, and while you shouldn't use it every day, you'll definitely want to keep some on hand. Bath milk is a gentle, suds-free option that's made for sensitive or dry skin.

moisturizers

If your baby has dry skin, there are lots of options available. On the lightest end of the spectrum is a moisturizing spray that's easy to rub in. In the middle are lotions and easily spreadable milk formulas. If you need a heavier moisturizer, try a cream or oil.

diaper cream

There are basically two types of diaper cream: those that protect against diaper rash (often known as barrier creams) and those intended to treat a rash. Either way, these creams come in a range of consistencies, from sheer balms to thicker creams to pastes. These may or may not include a zinc oxide barrier to protect your child against moisture for longer durations.

sunscreens
Children under the age of one need extra sun protection because of their thin and sensitive skin. Kid-formula sunscreens come in both lotions and light sprays, and a sunscreen stick is a quick and easy way to protect your baby's face.

general guidance
Sensitive care is especially important for babies, but it's a good habit to continue even for toddlers. Here are some terms to look for and what they mean.

- gentle: fewer chemicals and less alcohol
- hypoallergenic: formulated against allergic reactions
- all-natural: contains no synthetic ingredients
- organic: made from certified organic ingredients

Most pediatricians agree that you should avoid products containing mineral oil, petroleum, and lanolin when possible. Parents should also be cautious of fragranced products. While many are hypoallergenic, perfumes affect babies differently, so fragrance-free is a safe default.

Products come in every price range. Some stores offer bulk discounts with case purchases or as part of a loyalty program during your first years of parenthood, when consumption of products is particularly high.

sunscreen tips for baby

Do babies wear sunscreen? You bet! Studies have shown that sun damage occurring early in childhood increases the potential risk of skin cancer later in life. And children under the age of one need extra sun protection because of their thin and sensitive skin, even if you're only going for a short stroll.

In addition to staying out of the midday sun and dressing your baby in protective clothing, the best way to protect your child is with a pure physical sunscreen. As opposed to chemical sunscreens, which absorb UV radiation on the skin and then disperse the energy into harmless rays, physical sunscreens sit on top of the skin, reflecting, scattering, and blocking UVA and UVB radiation.

Only physical sunscreens (or combination sunscreens, which offer both physical and chemical blocks) have broad-spectrum UVA and UVB coverage, which means they give you the best protection available. Physical sunscreens are also less irritating, since they don't get absorbed into the top layer of skin.

Chemical and physical sunscreens contain different ingredients, and the best way to tell you're getting a physical sunscreen is to look for zinc oxide or titanium dioxide on the label. If you do use a chemical sunscreen, apply it half an hour before going outside so it has a chance to absorb, and make sure it's PABA-free.

Whichever you choose, shoot for an SPF of at least 30. Anything less doesn't offer enough protection, and anything more doesn't really make that big of a difference, as long as you're applying it as directed. Be generous with the sunscreen, and don't overlook smaller areas like ears, nose, and back of neck. If you're using a spray-on sunscreen, spray up close to make sure it doesn't dissipate before making it to the skin.

features to look for

tearless. Try as you might to avoid it, soap and shampoo will eventually get in your baby's eyes, so look for tearless formulas that won't sting.

special formulas. If your child has eczema or extra-sensitive skin, look for formulas that are made to help—some are now available without a prescription.

usage tips

• Most babies will have some form of dry skin not long after birth as their skin adjusts to the outside world. Lotions may or may not help, but if the condition persists, talk to your pediatrician.

• Some formulas are concentrated, so only a little is required. Read your product instructions carefully.

• Don't fret if your baby gets acne during the first couple of months. With patience, time, and gentle, warm-water cleaning, it will disappear as quickly as it appeared.

accessories

hand-wipes. These are useful to have around to clean your hands after you've applied sunscreen.

belly-button swabs. Plain cotton swabs or predipped alcohol swabs help with the daily care of a healing umbilical cord.

resources

The American Academy of Pediatrics
1-847-434-4000
www.aap.org

National Highway Traffic Safety Administration
1-888-DASH-2-DOT
www.nhtsa.dot.gov

Juvenile Products Manufacturers' Association
1-856-638-0420
www.jpma.org

The American Society for Testing and Materials
1-610-832-9585
www.astm.org

Consumer Reports
www.consumerreports.org

First Candle/SIDS Alliance
1-800-221-7437
www.sidsalliance.org

To learn more about co-sleeping, visit www.cosleeping.org.

acknowledgments

Special thanks to everyone who helped make this book what it is, starting with my giggle customers, who ask all the right questions and have helped me understand what's most important to new parents.

I'd also like to thank my vendors, not only for their support, but for their focused product expertise.

Thanks to my wonderful and talented team for committing to giggle being a learning company that's always open to feedback, growth, and the "better way."

As for the book itself, thanks to Mariella for her terrific prose and persistence, and to Lisa Campbell and Chronicle Books for their editing, support, and vision.

And most especially, thanks to my family for their love, support, and sacrifice of family time required for my many (many!) hours spent studying this market.